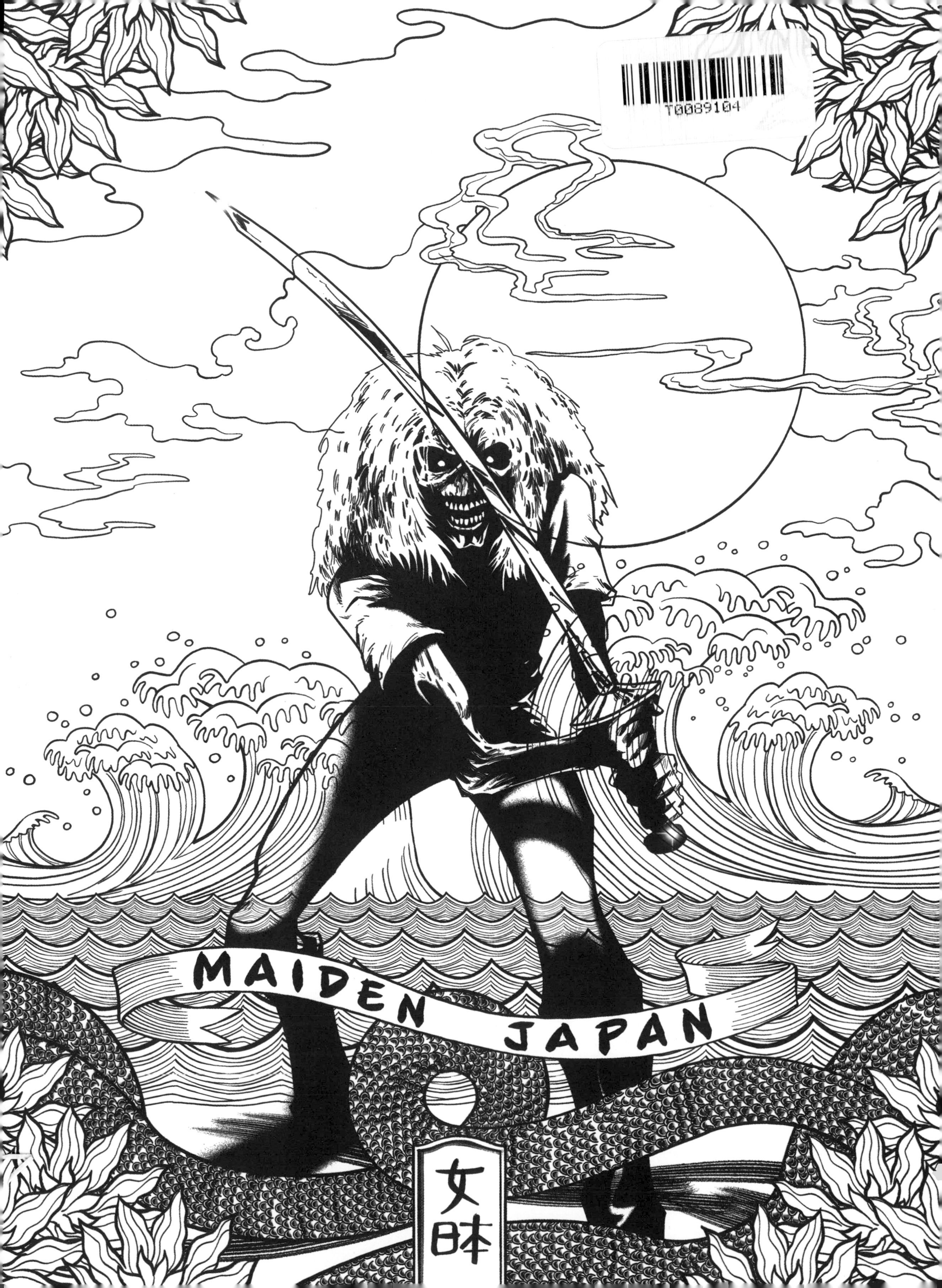
MAIDEN
JAPAN
女
日本

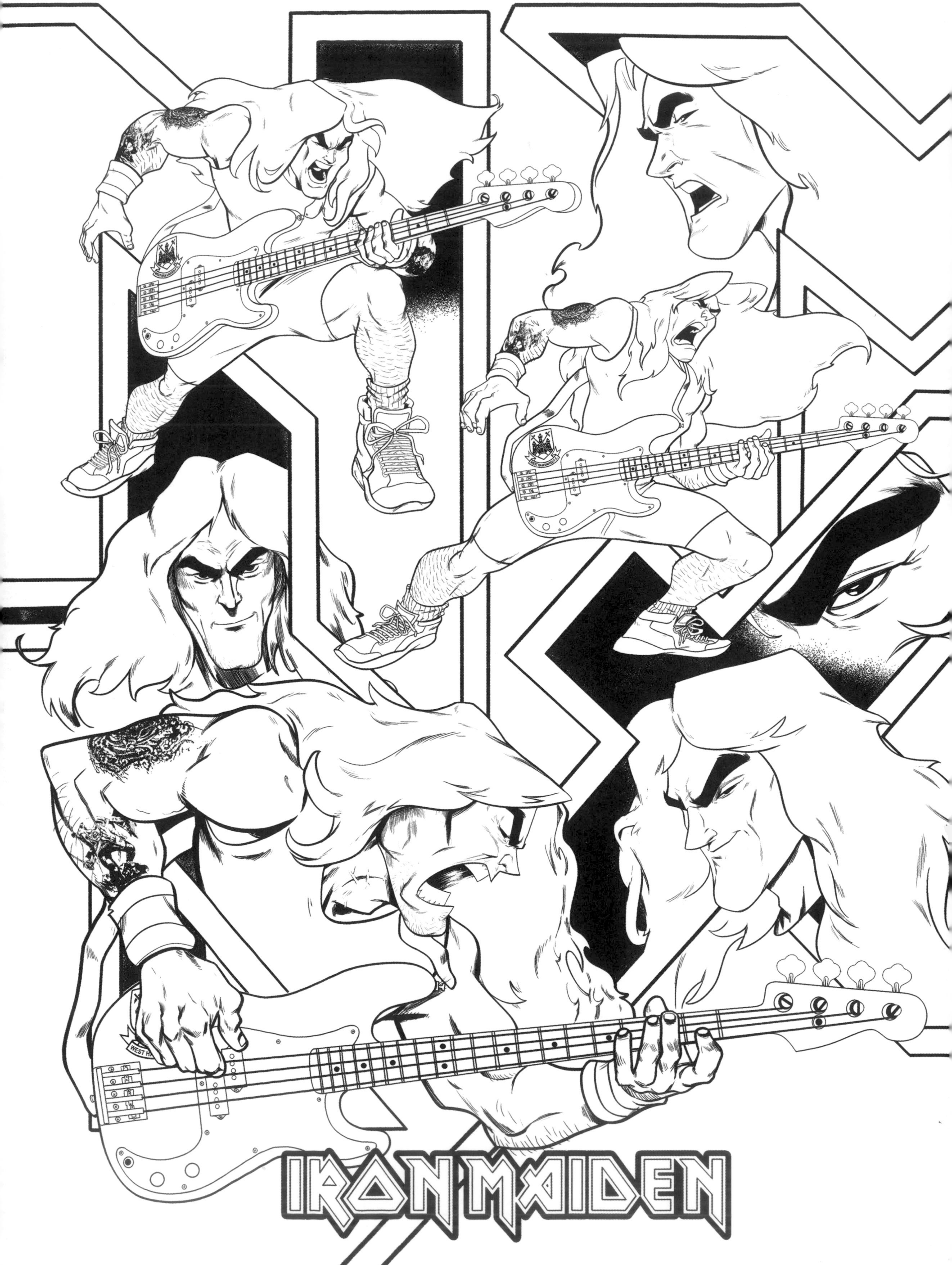
IRON MAIDEN

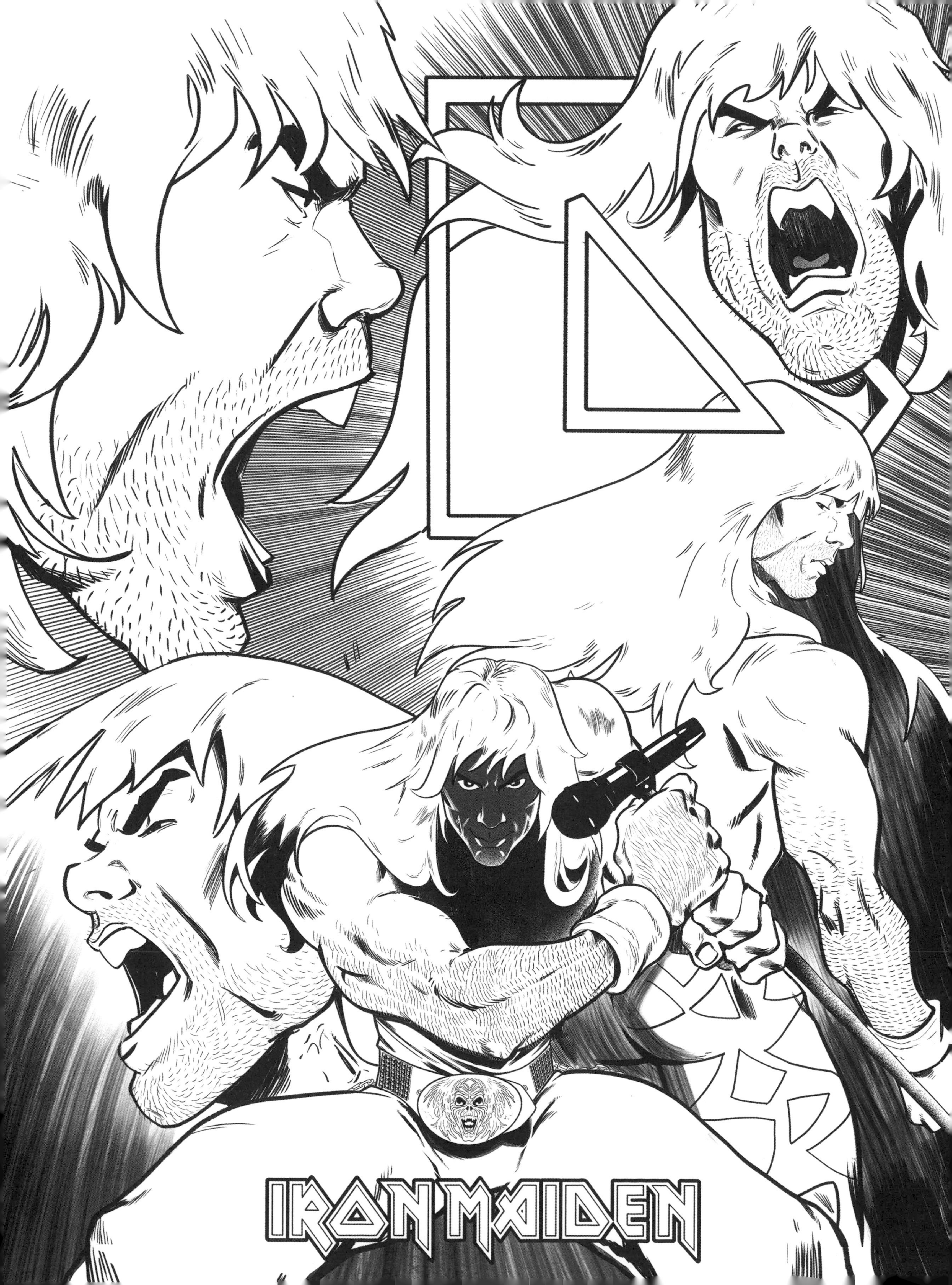
IRON MAIDEN

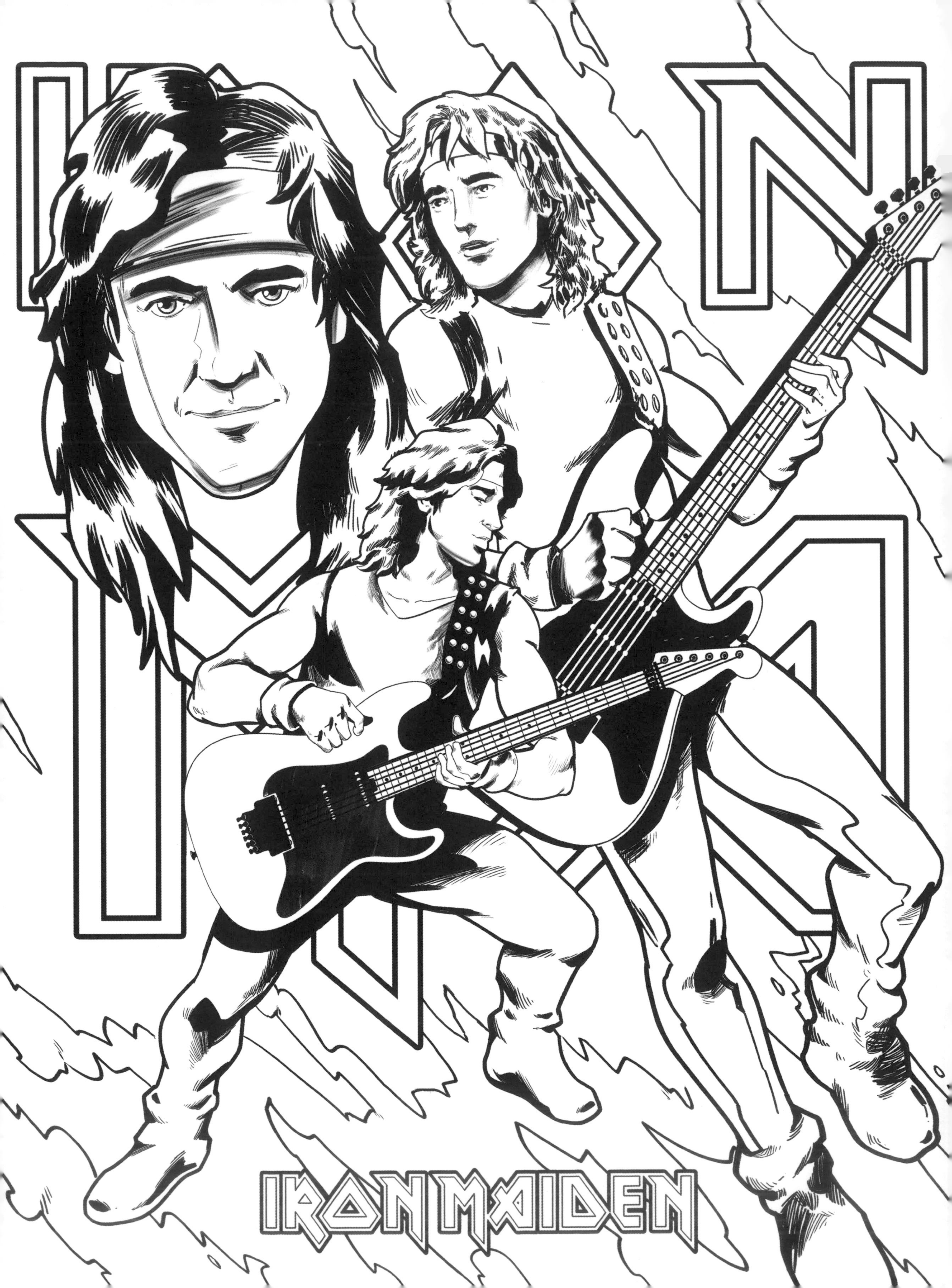
IRONMAIDEN

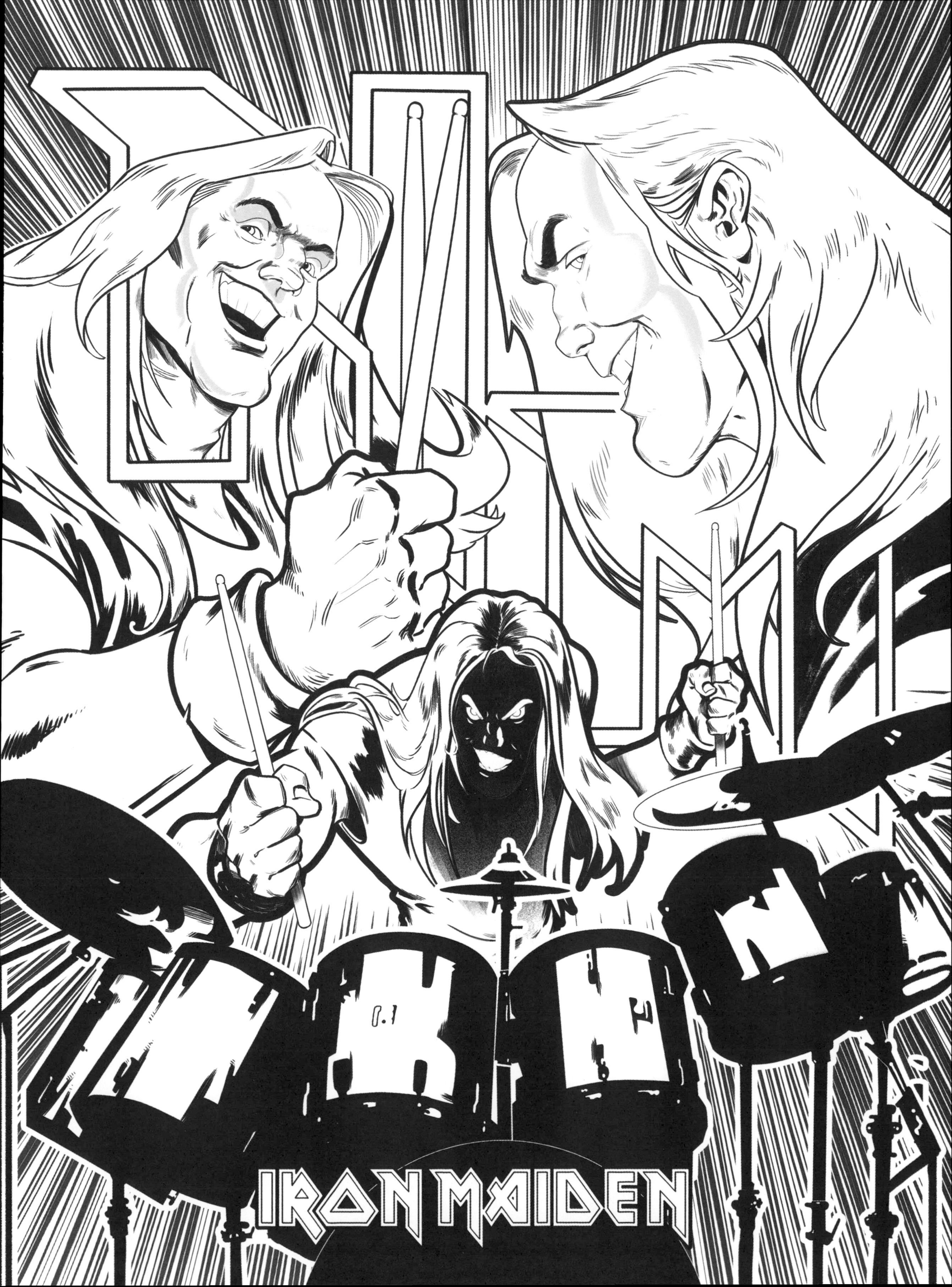
IRON MAIDEN

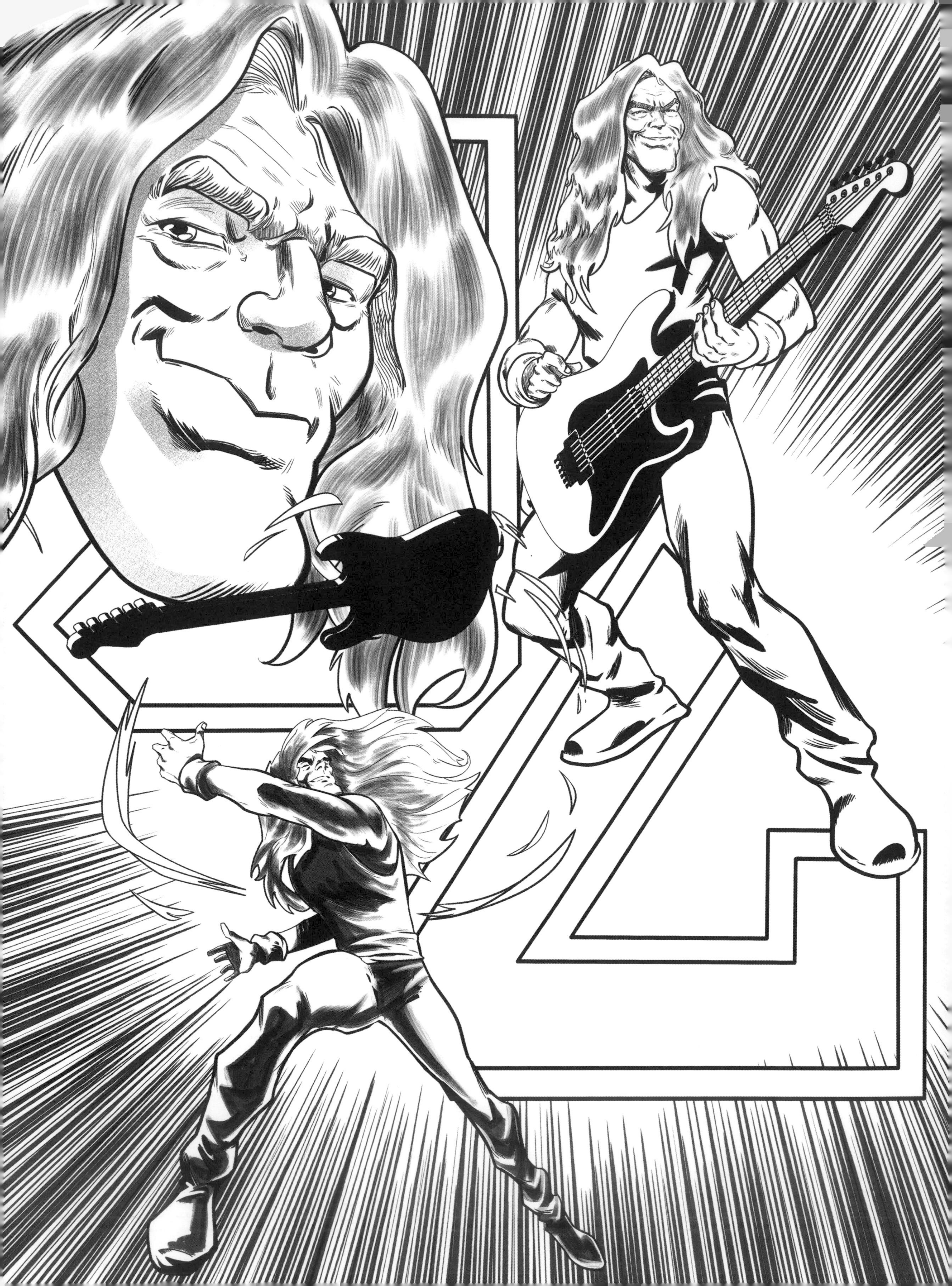

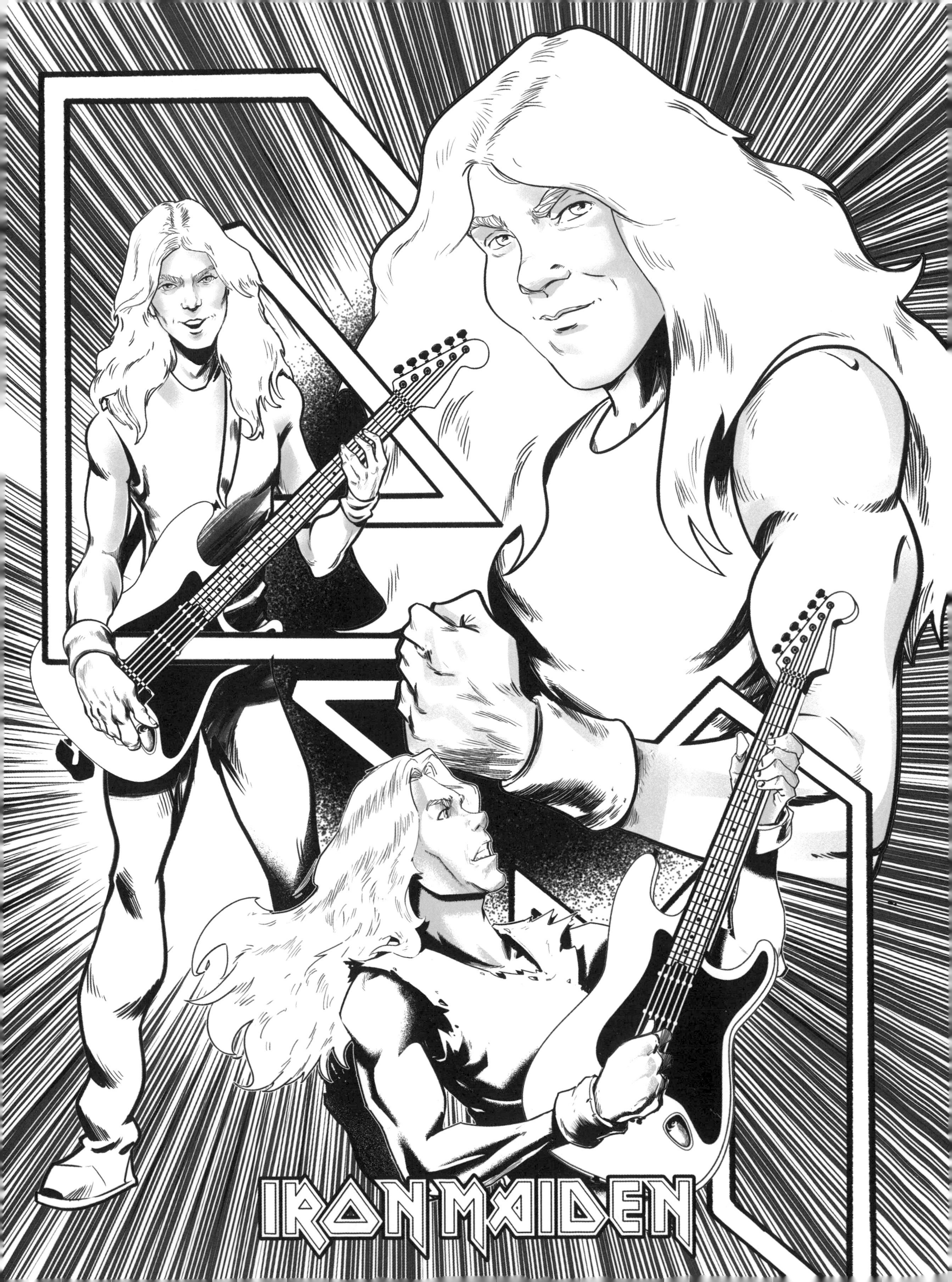
IRON MAIDEN

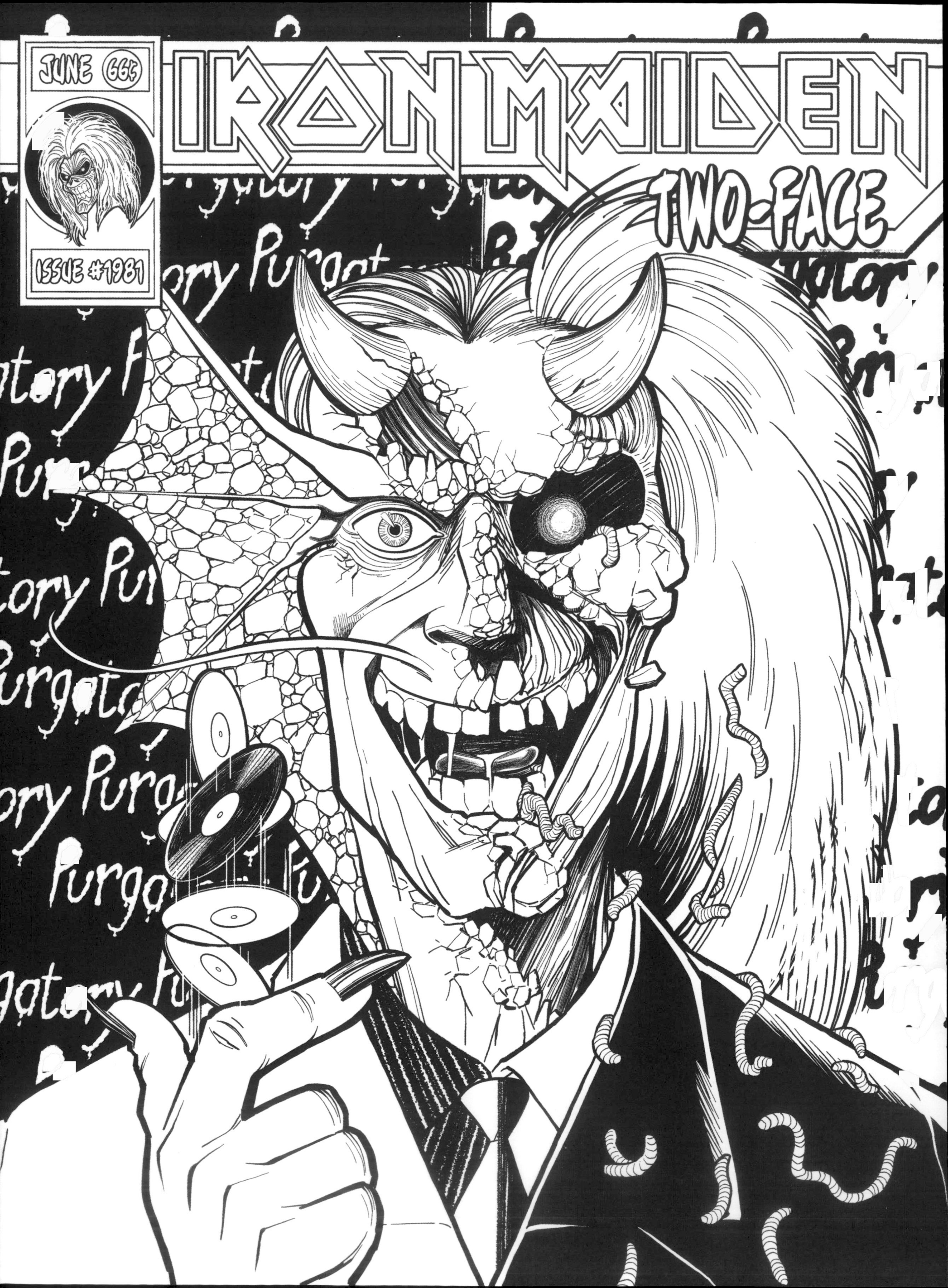
JUNE 666
IRON MAIDEN
TWO-FACE
ISSUE #1981

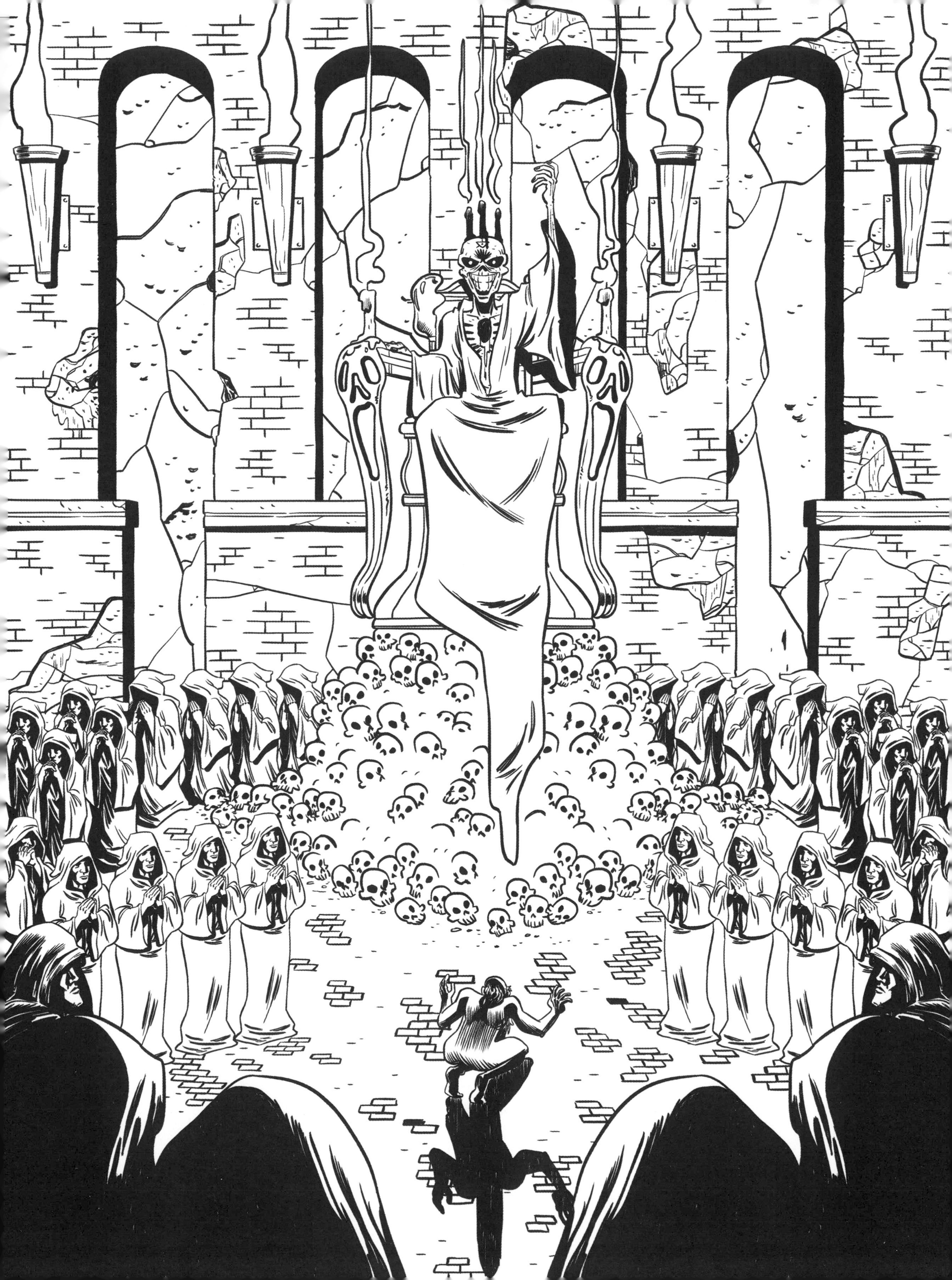

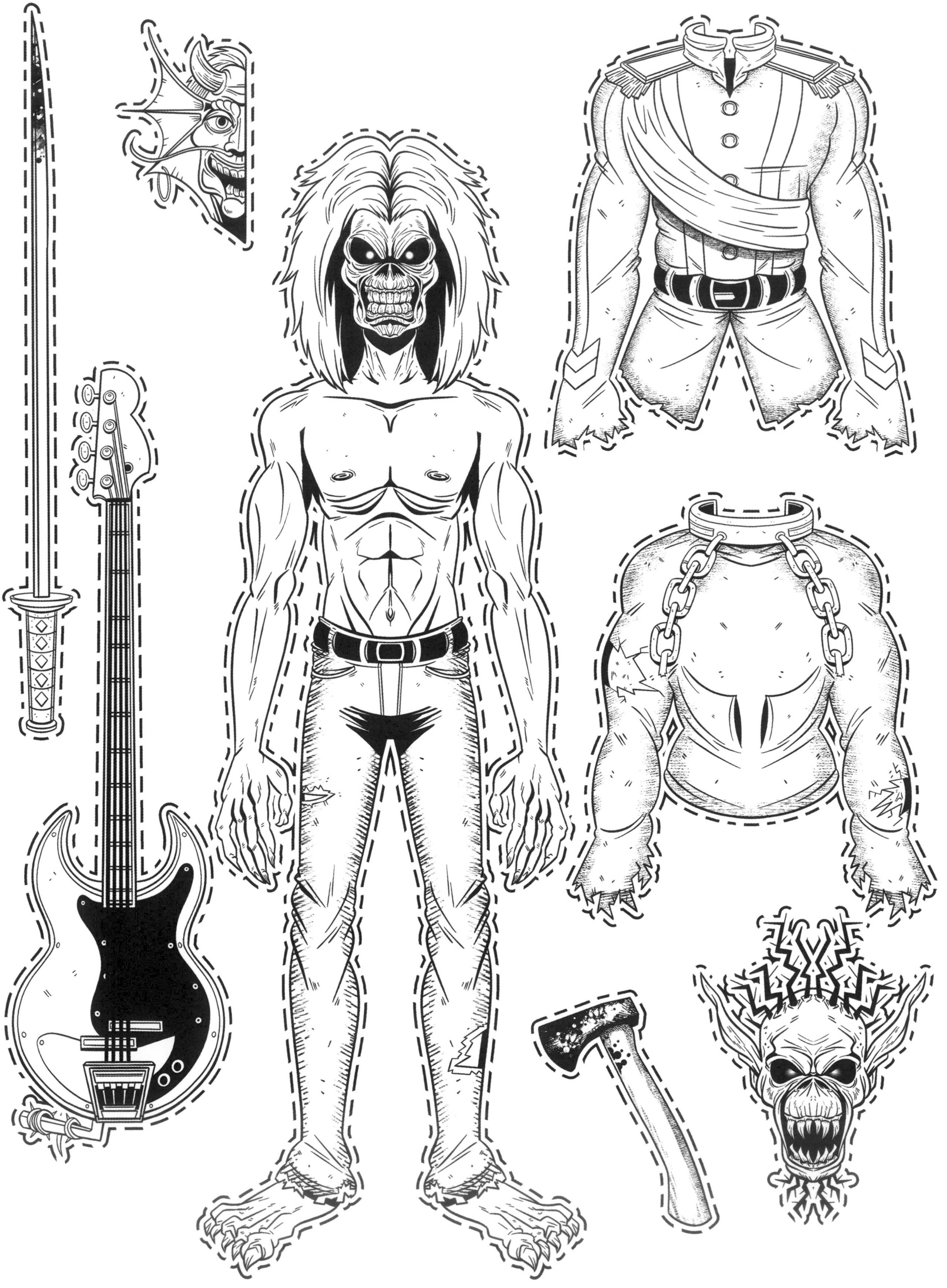

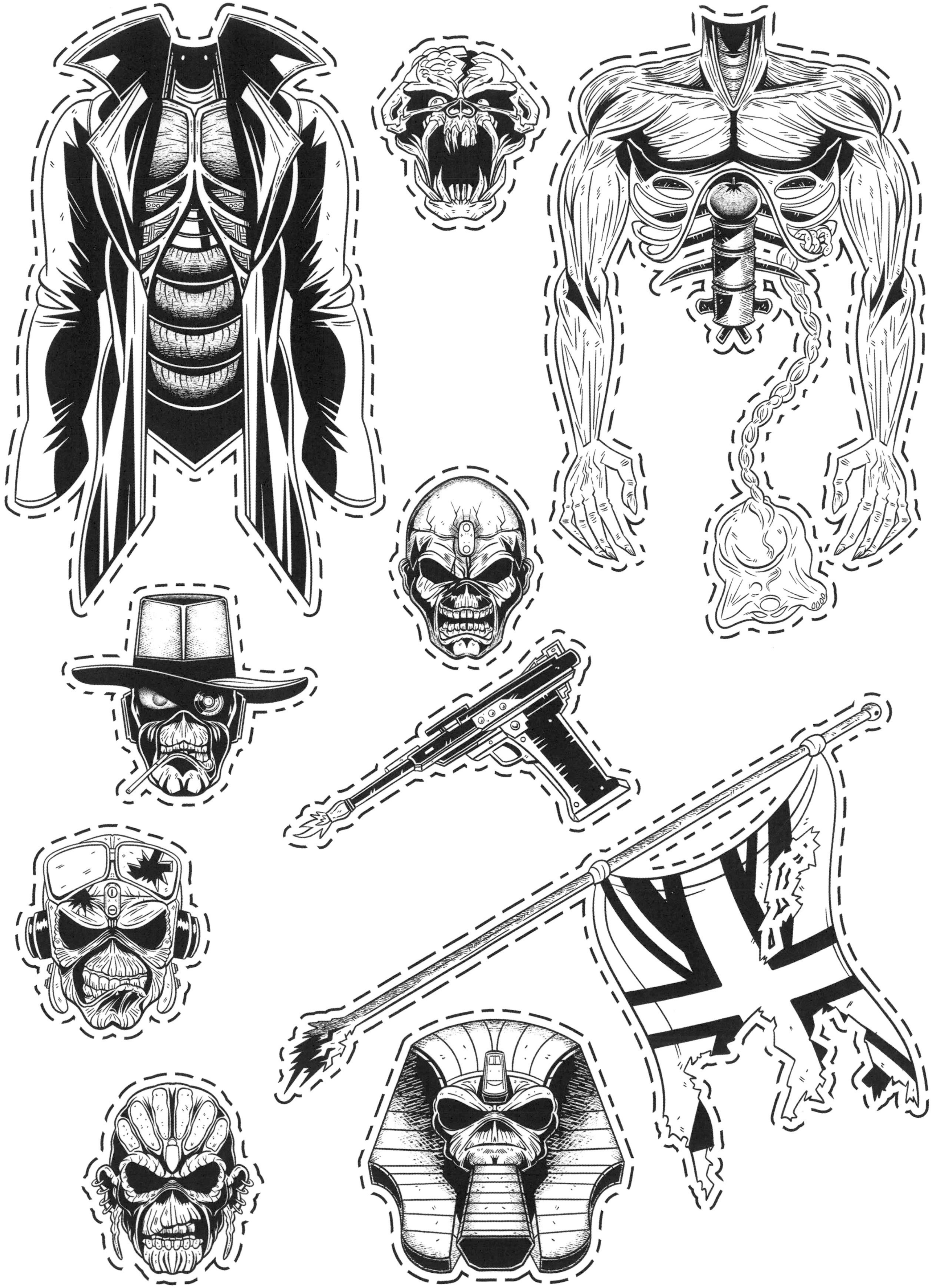

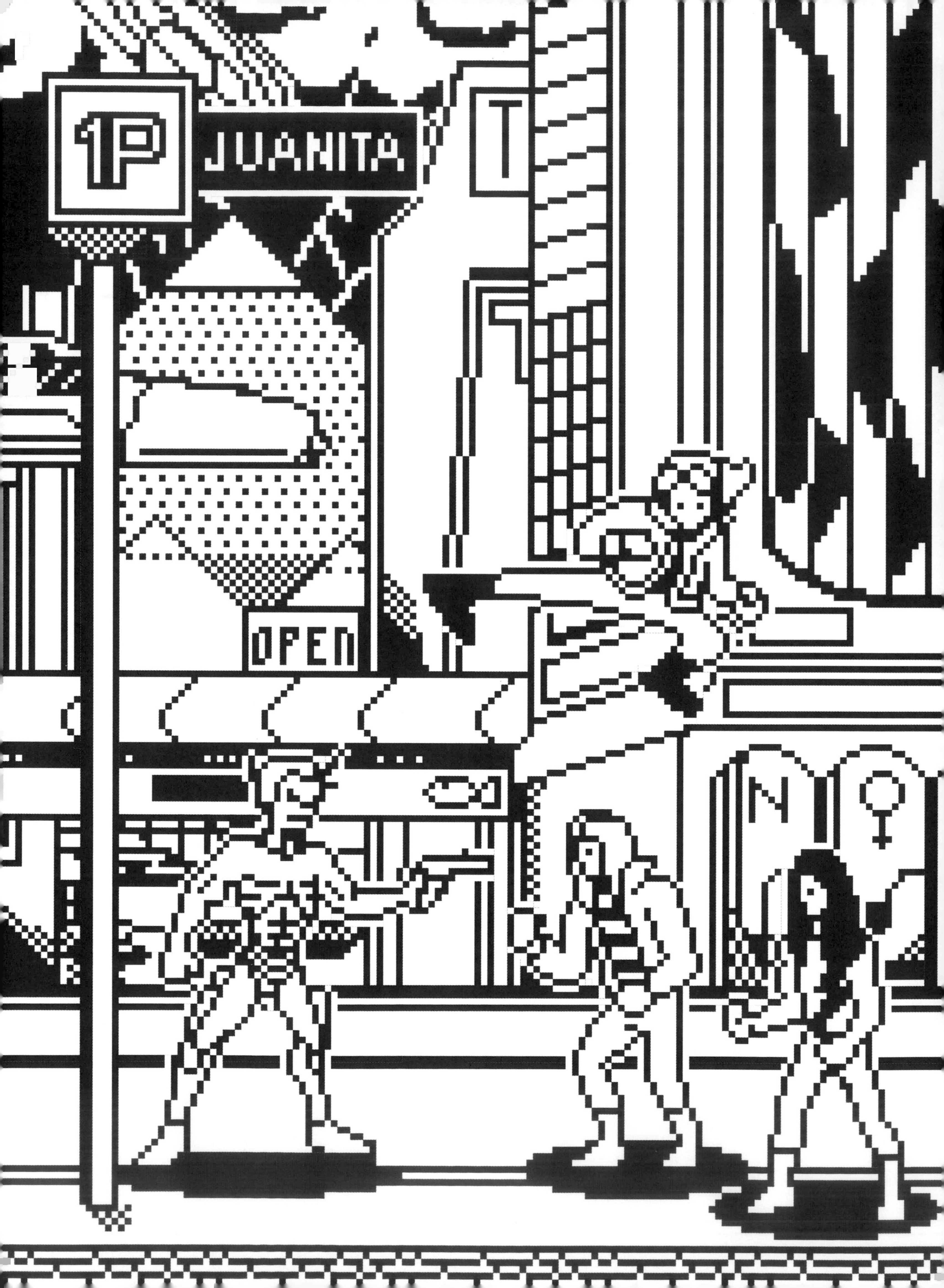
1P
JUANITA
T
OPEN
NO

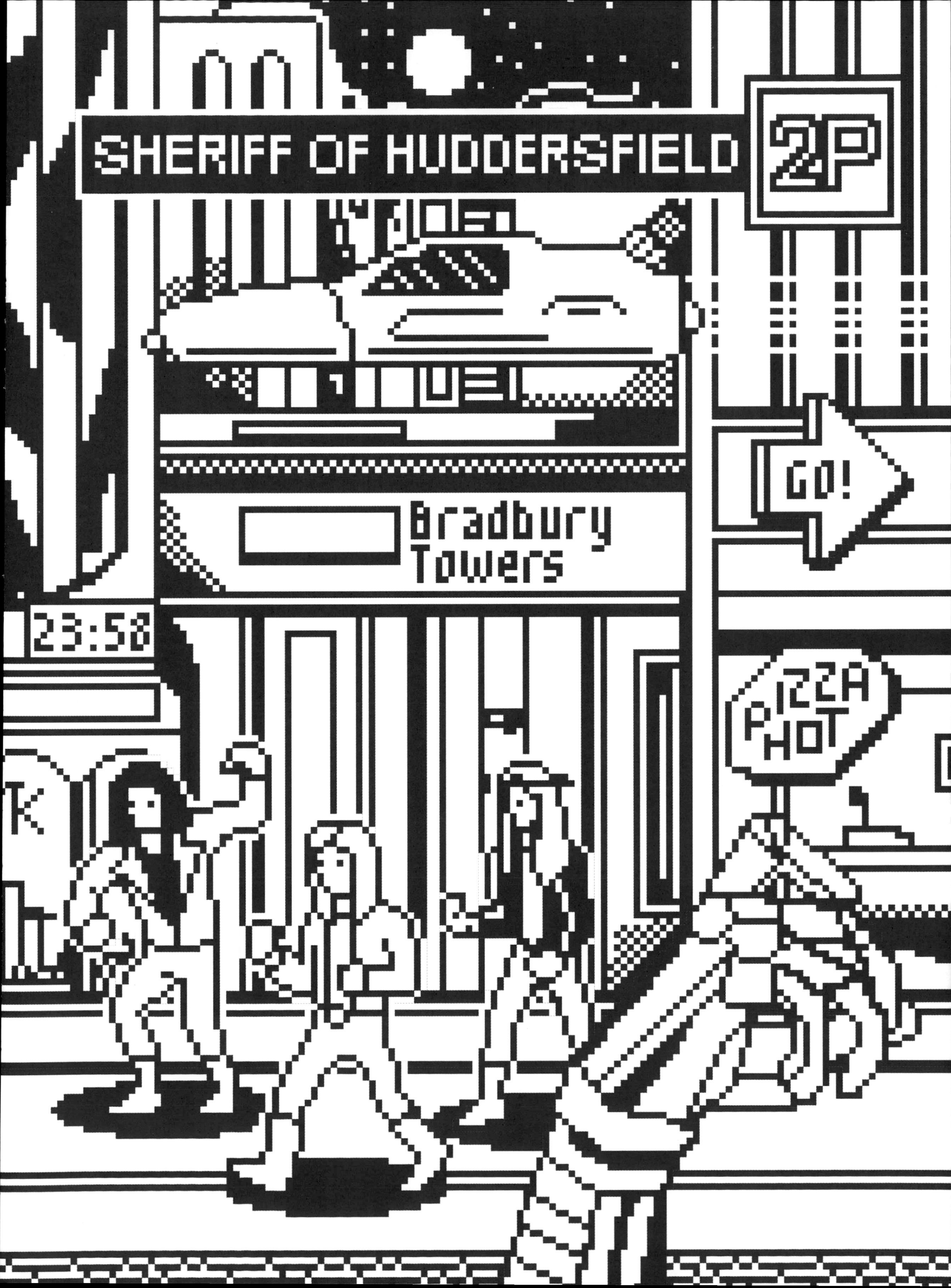
SHERIFF OF HUDDERSFIELD
2P
GO!
Bradbury
Towers
23:58
PIZZA
HOT

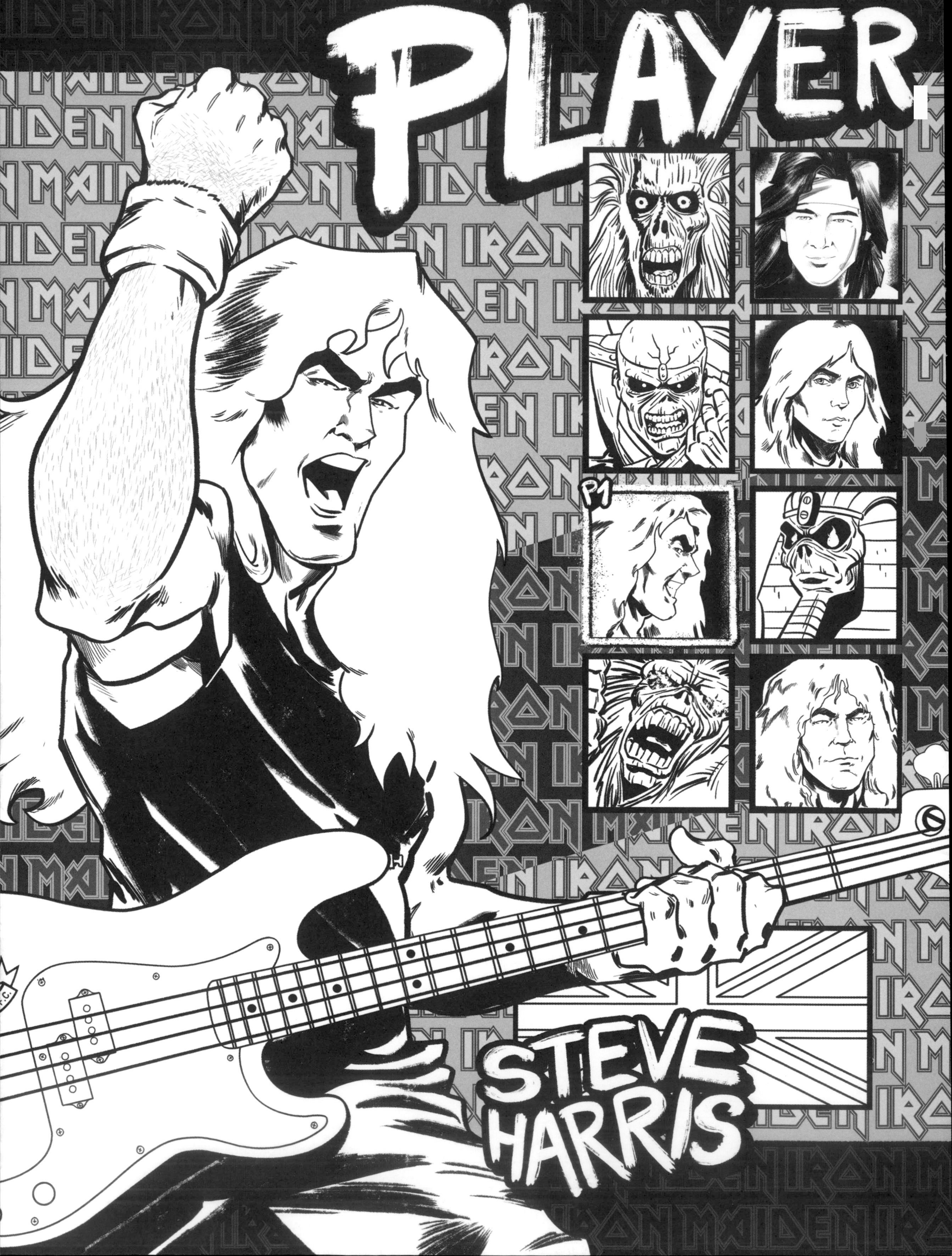
PLAYER 1
P1
STEVE HARRIS

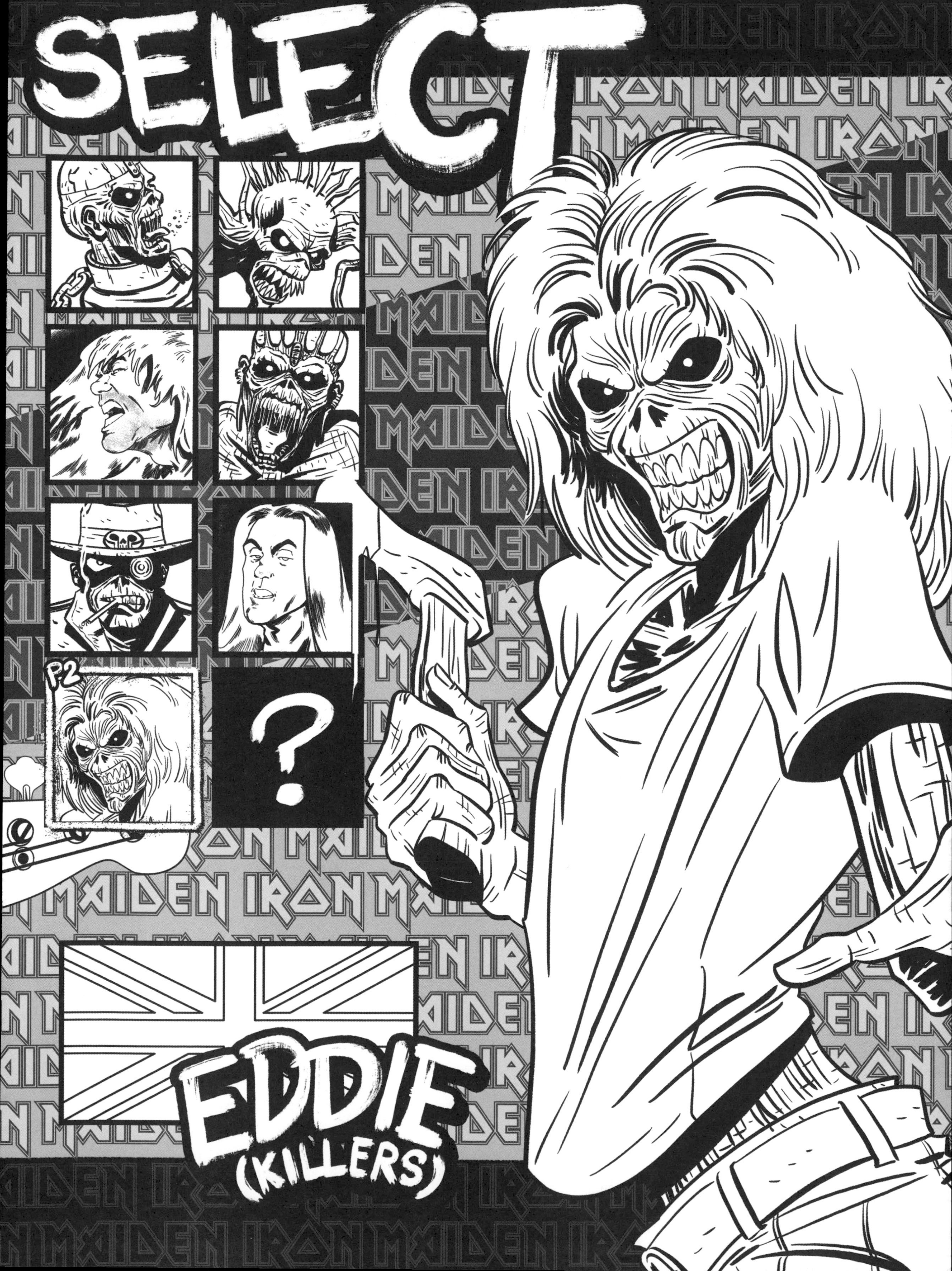
SELECT
P2
?
EDDIE
(KILLERS)

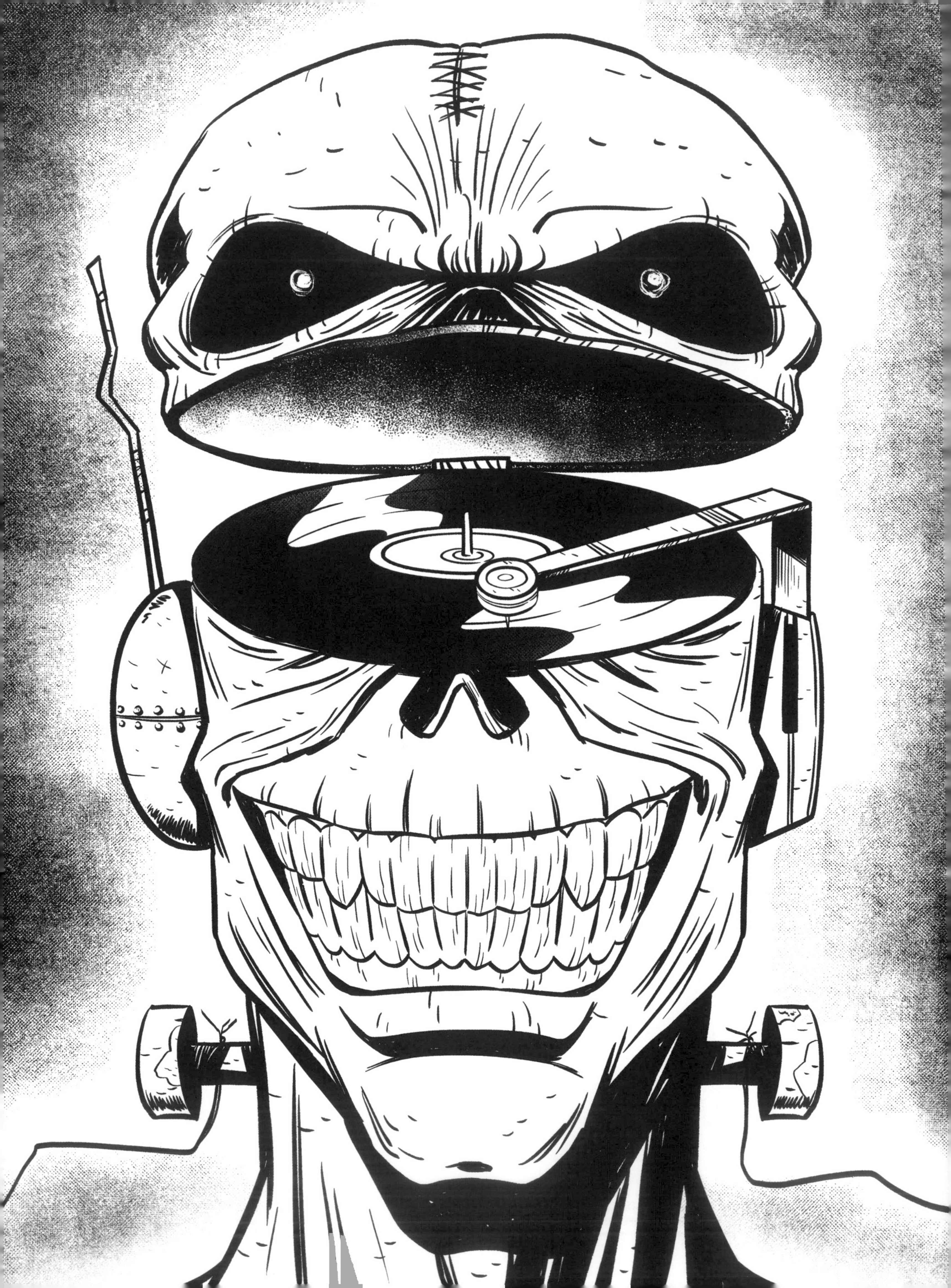

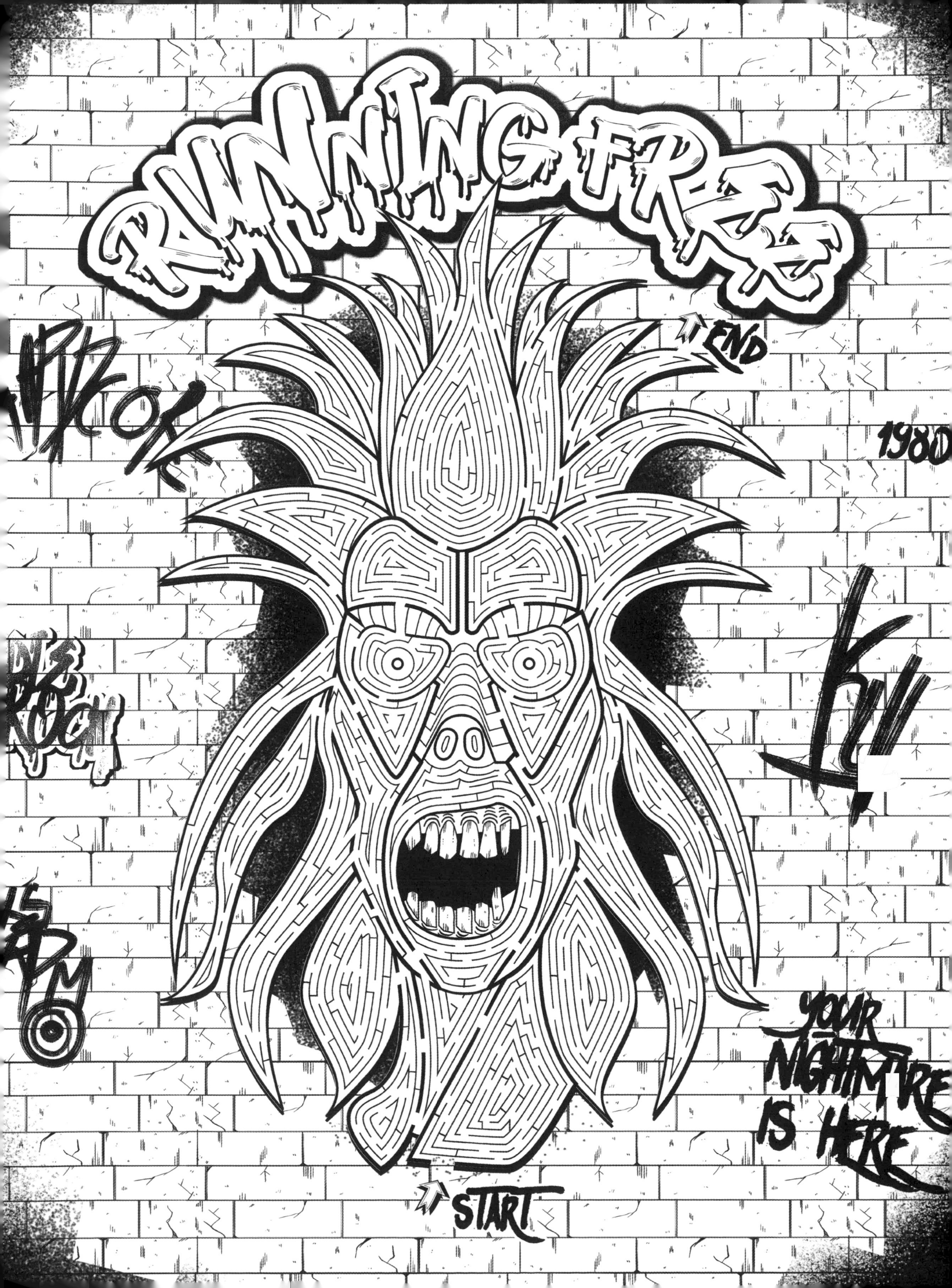
RUNNING FREE
END
1980
START
YOUR NIGHTMARE IS HERE

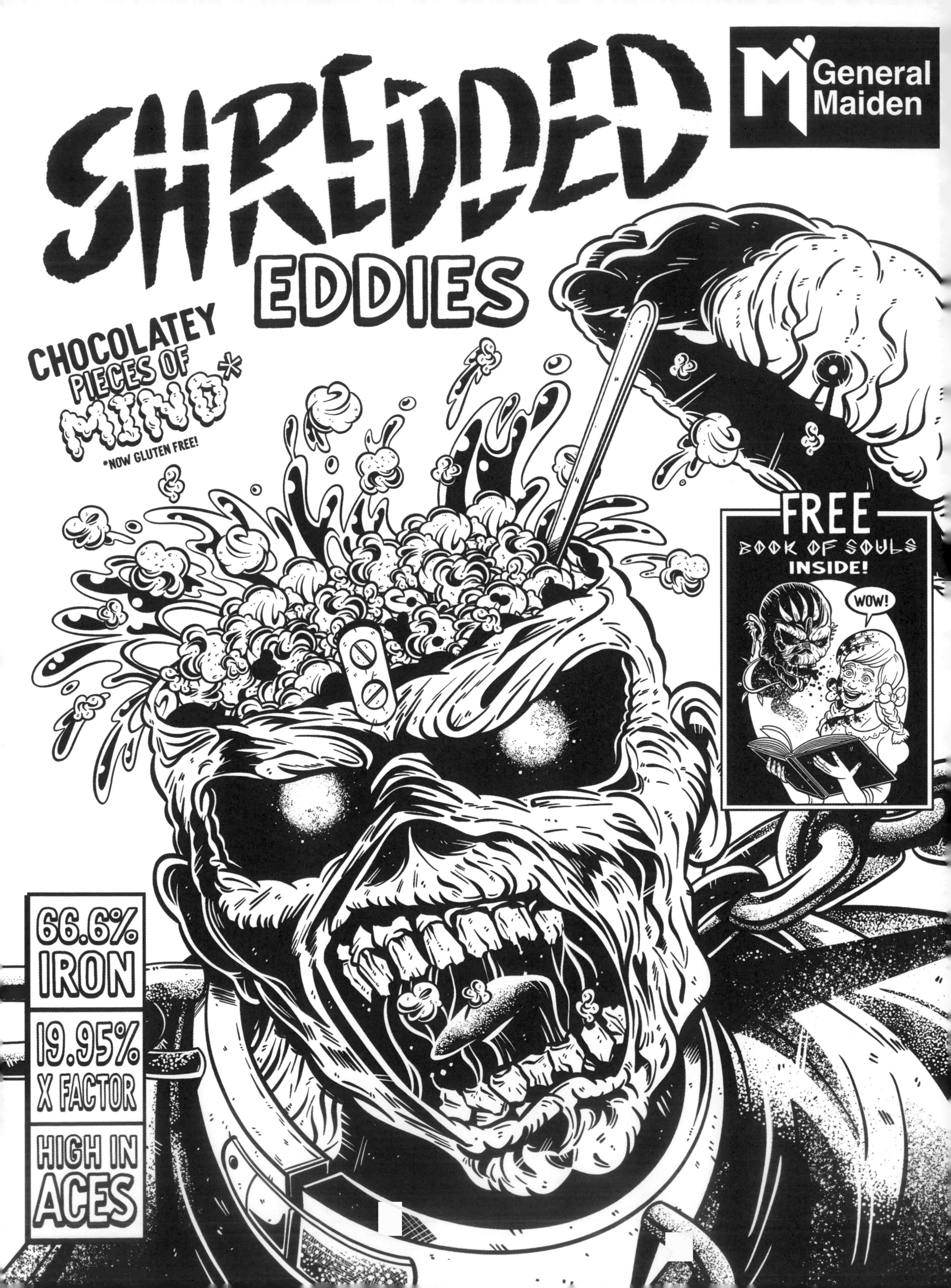
SHREDDED
EDDIES
General Maiden
CHOCOLATEY
PIECES OF
MIND*
*NOW GLUTEN FREE!
FREE
BOOK OF SOULS
INSIDE!
WOW!
66.6%
IRON
19.95%
X FACTOR
HIGH IN
ACES

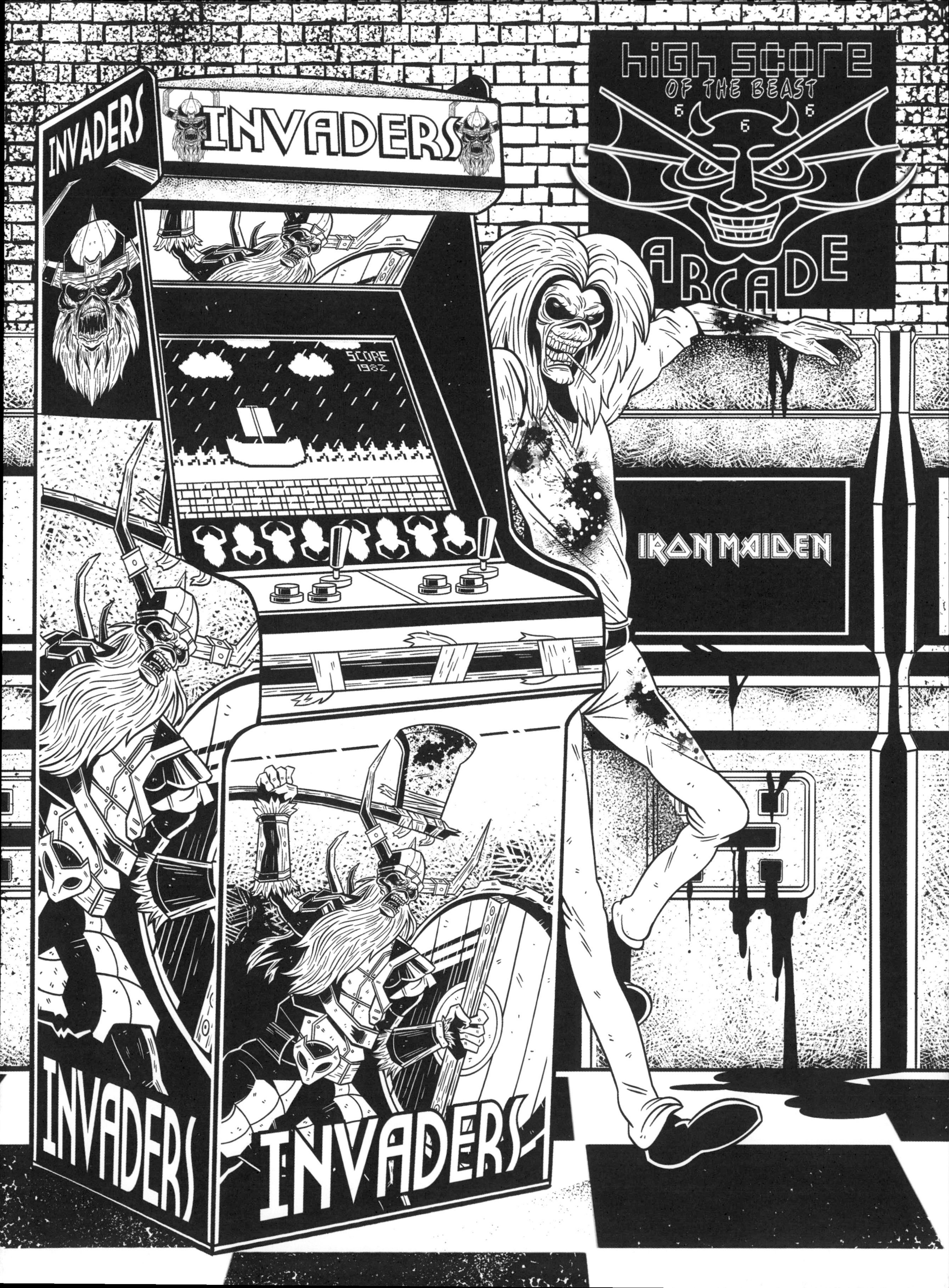

INVADERS
INVADERS
SCORE
1982
hiGh SCORE
OF THE BEAST
6
6
6
ARCADE
IRON MAIDEN
INVADERS
INVADERS

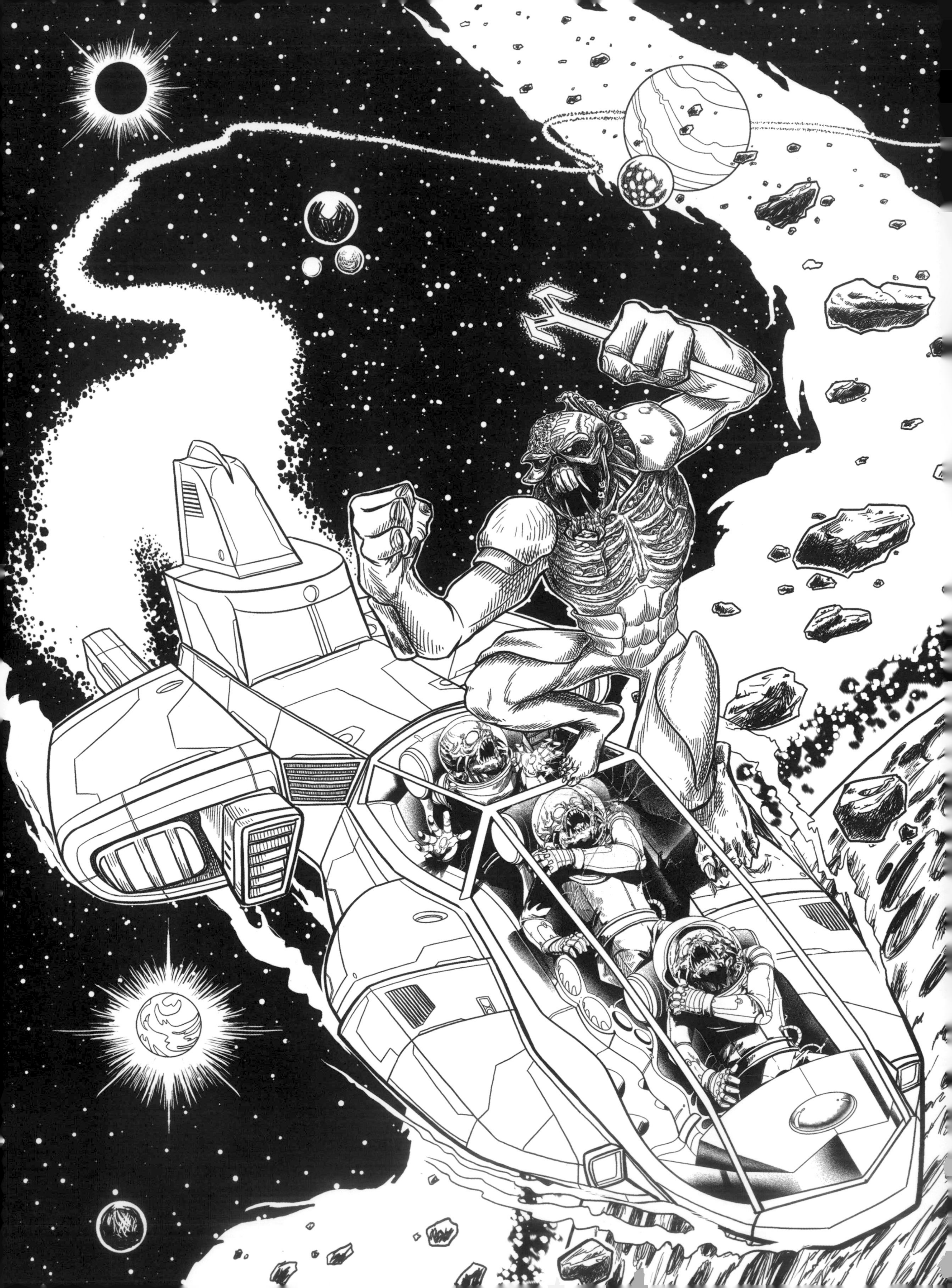

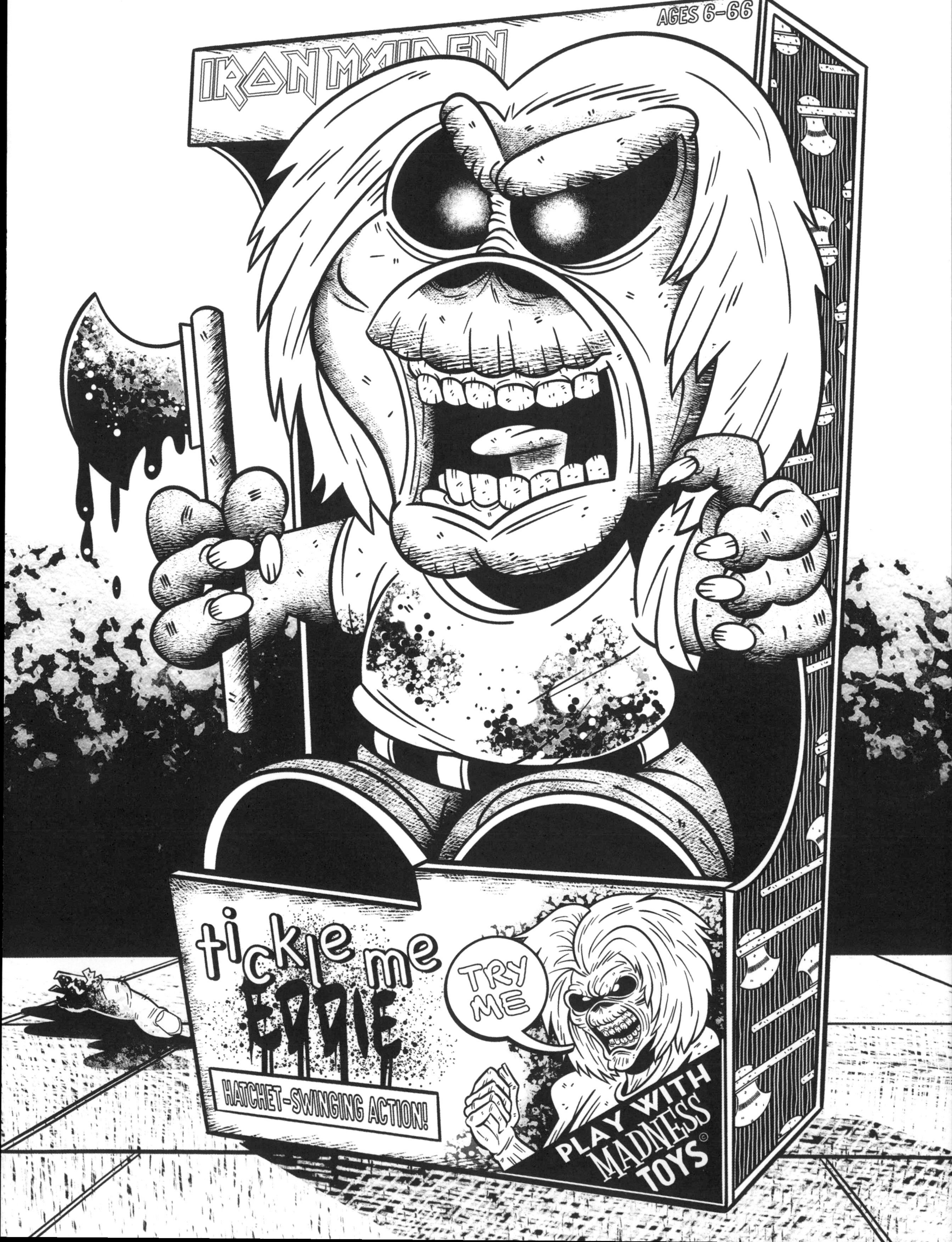
AGES 6-66
IRON MAIDEN
tickle me
EDDIE
HATCHET-SWINGING ACTION!
TRY ME
PLAY WITH
MADNESS
TOYS ©

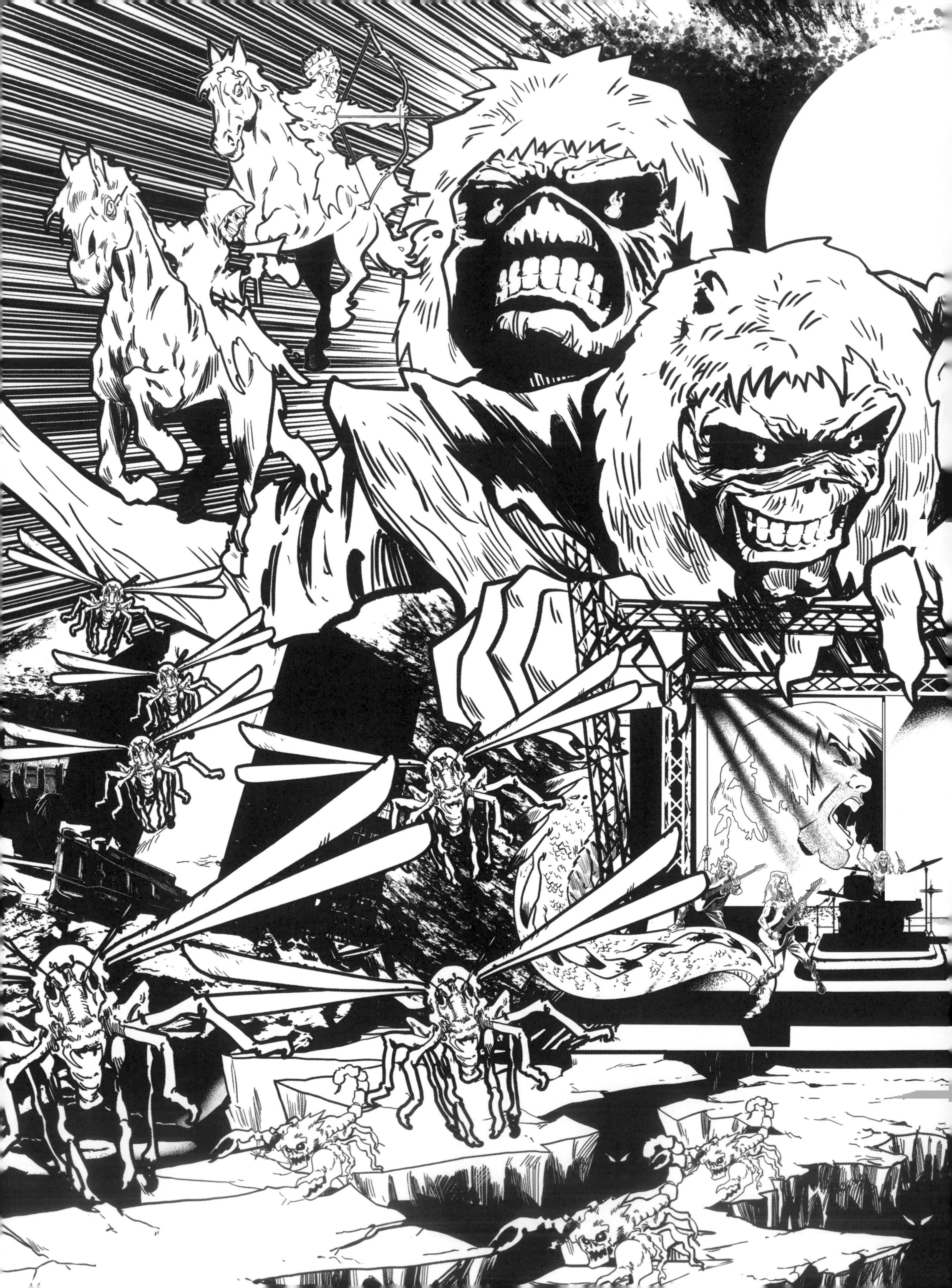

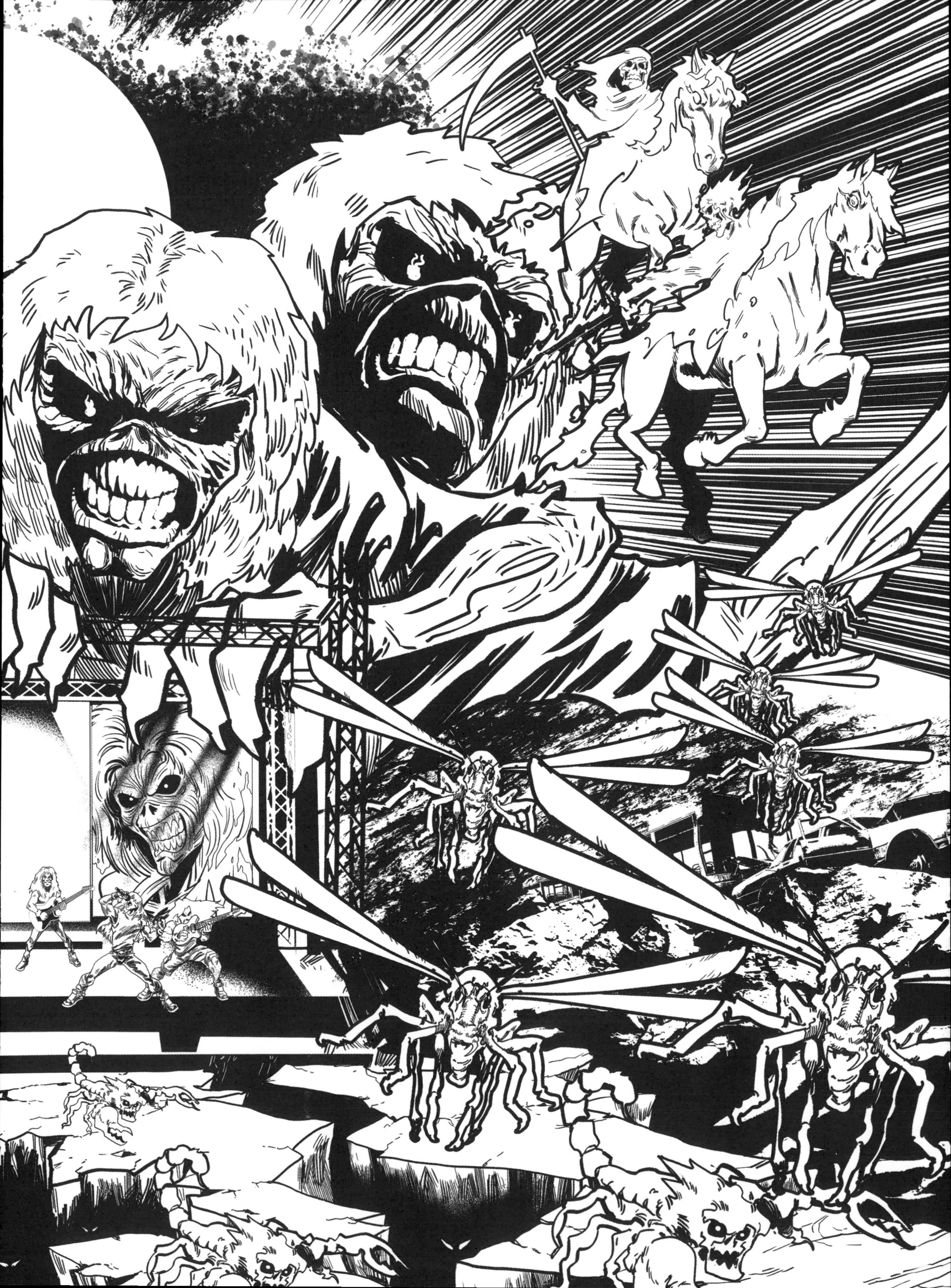

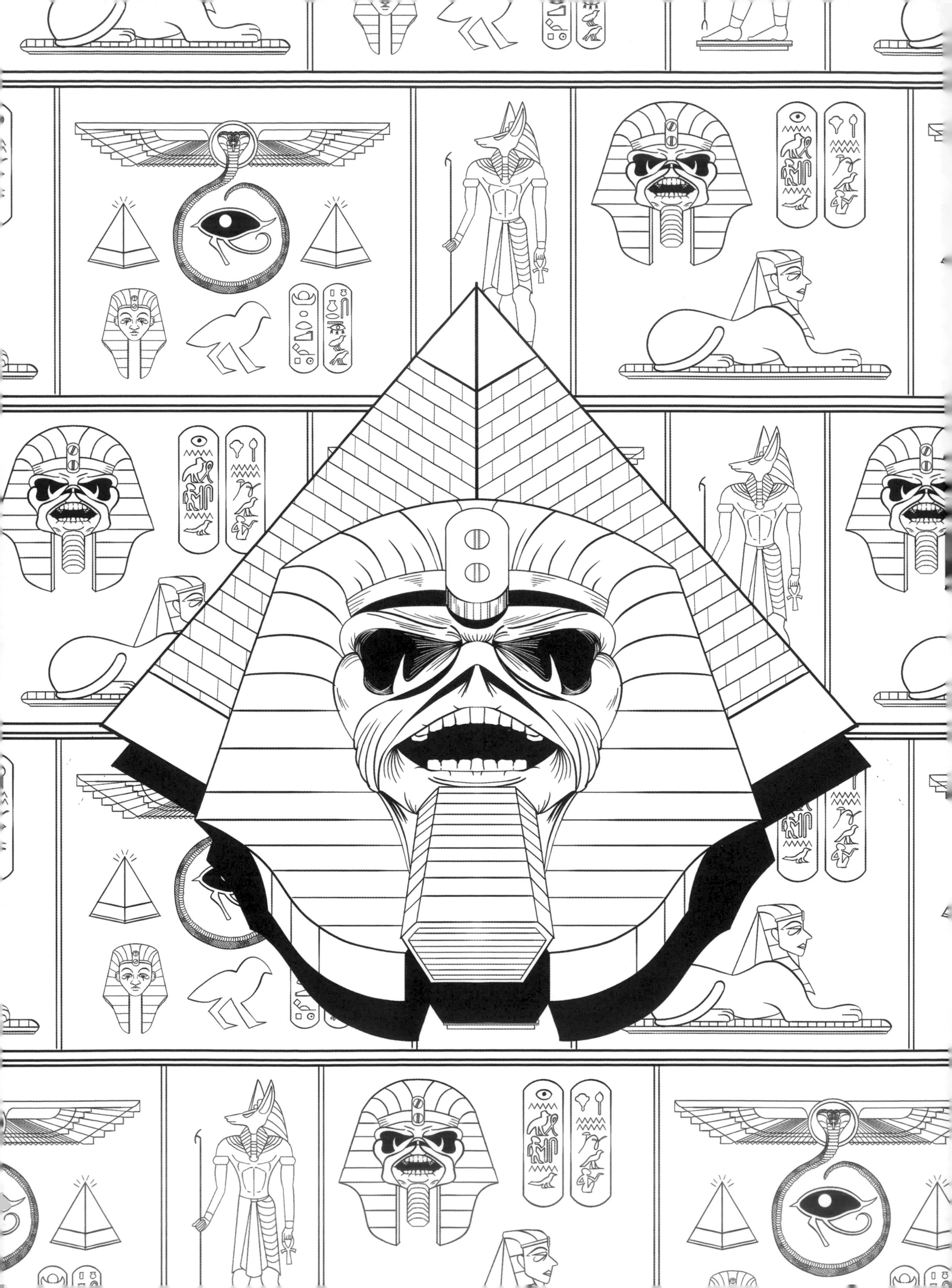

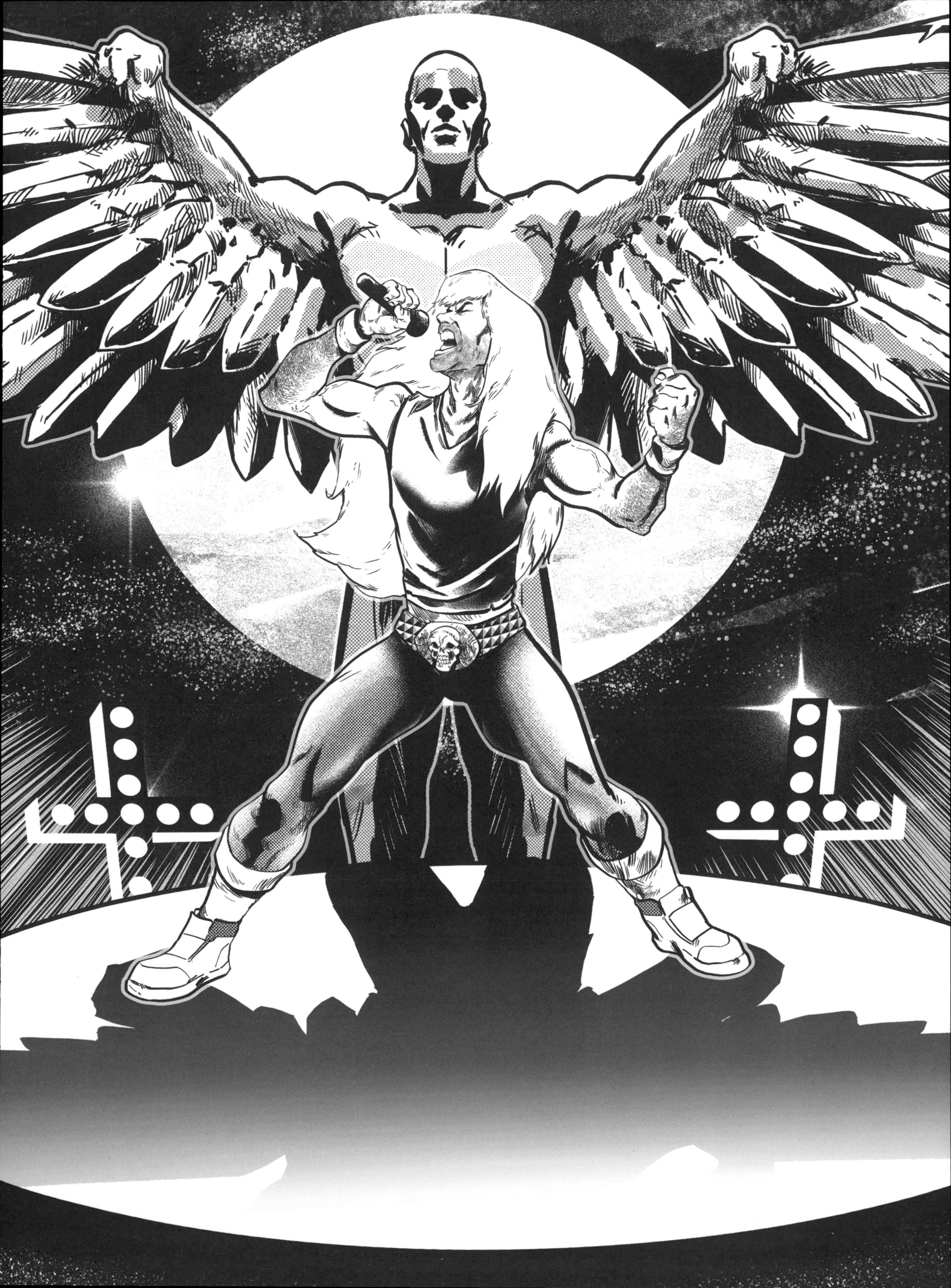

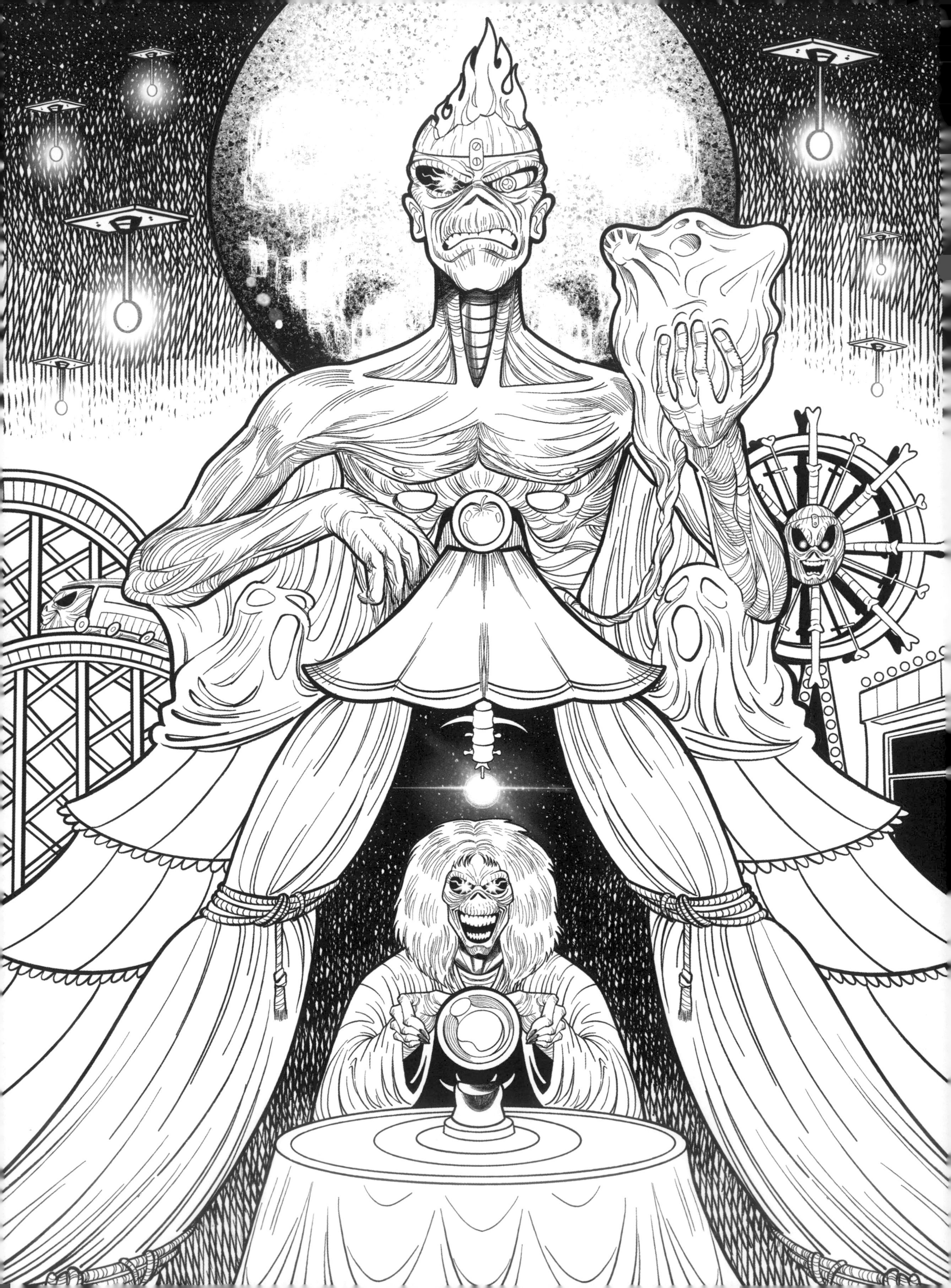

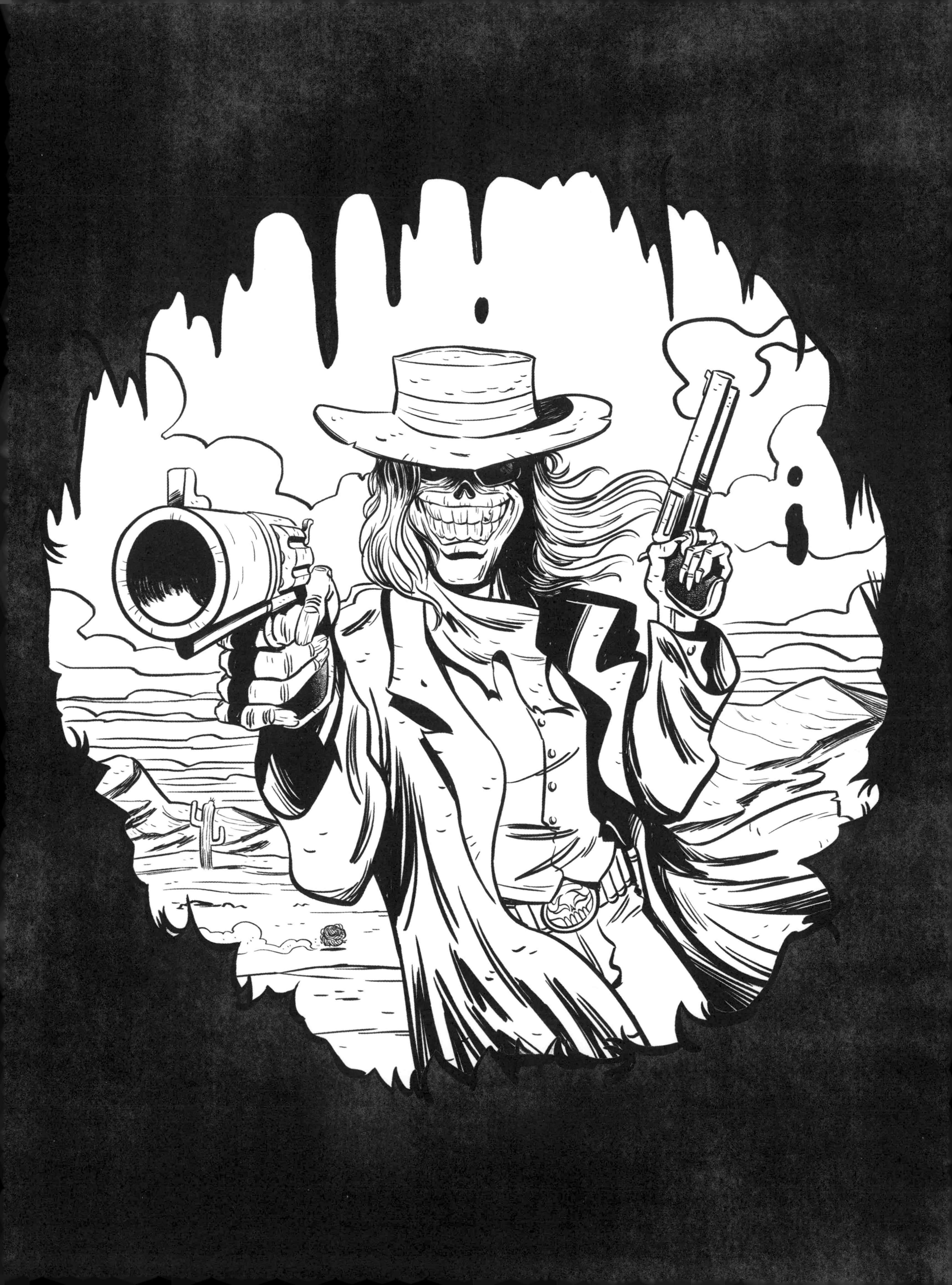

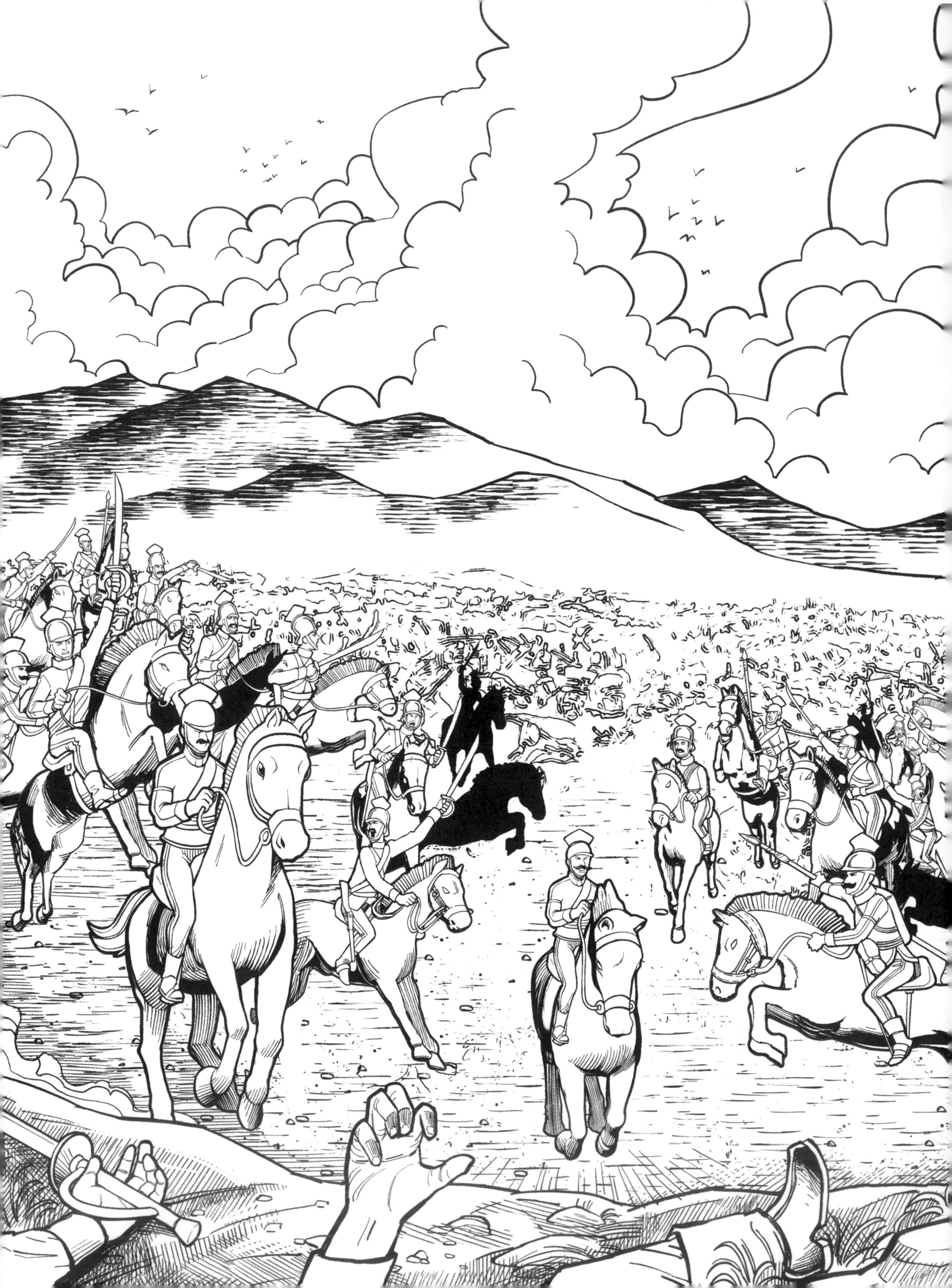

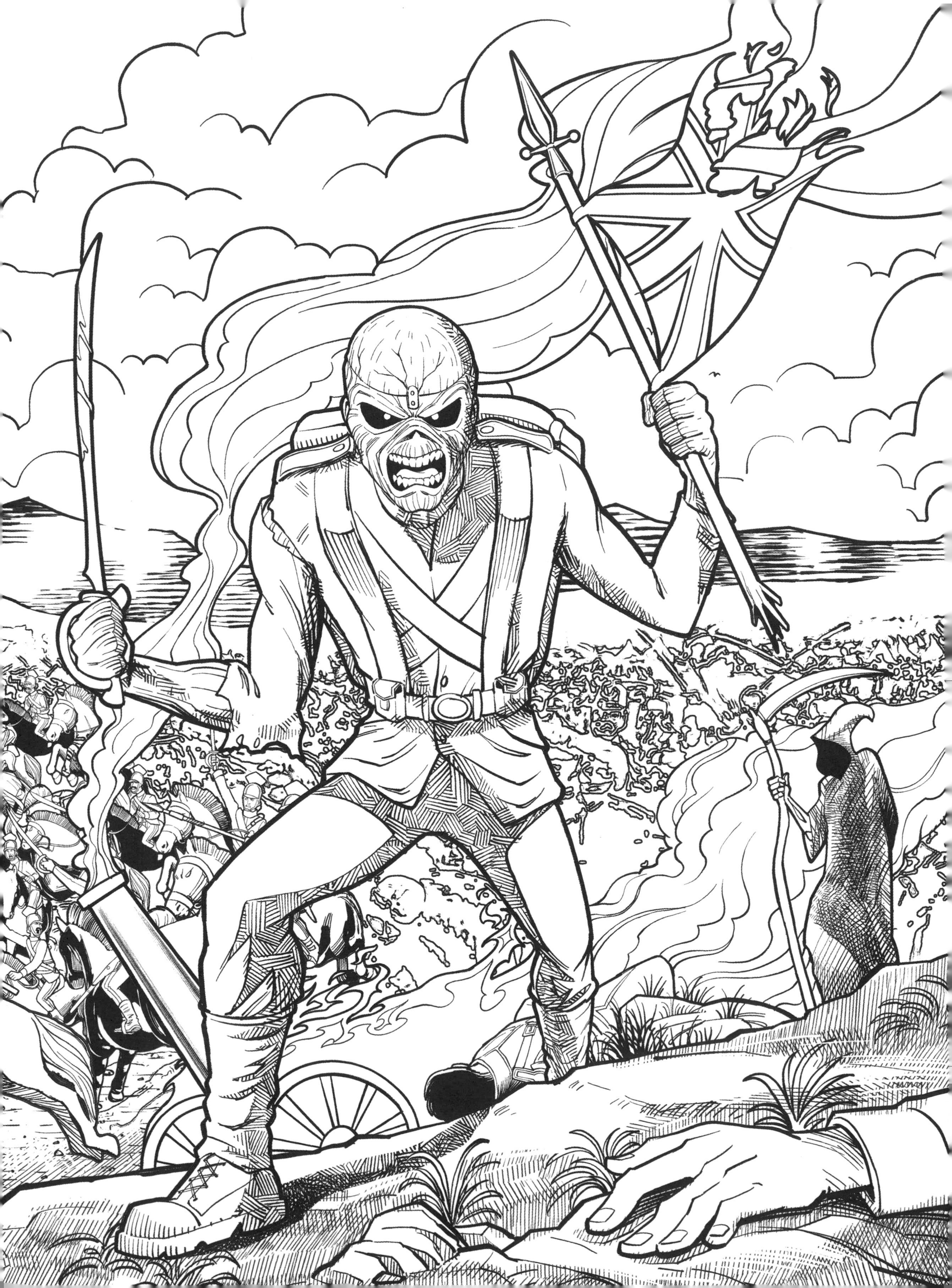

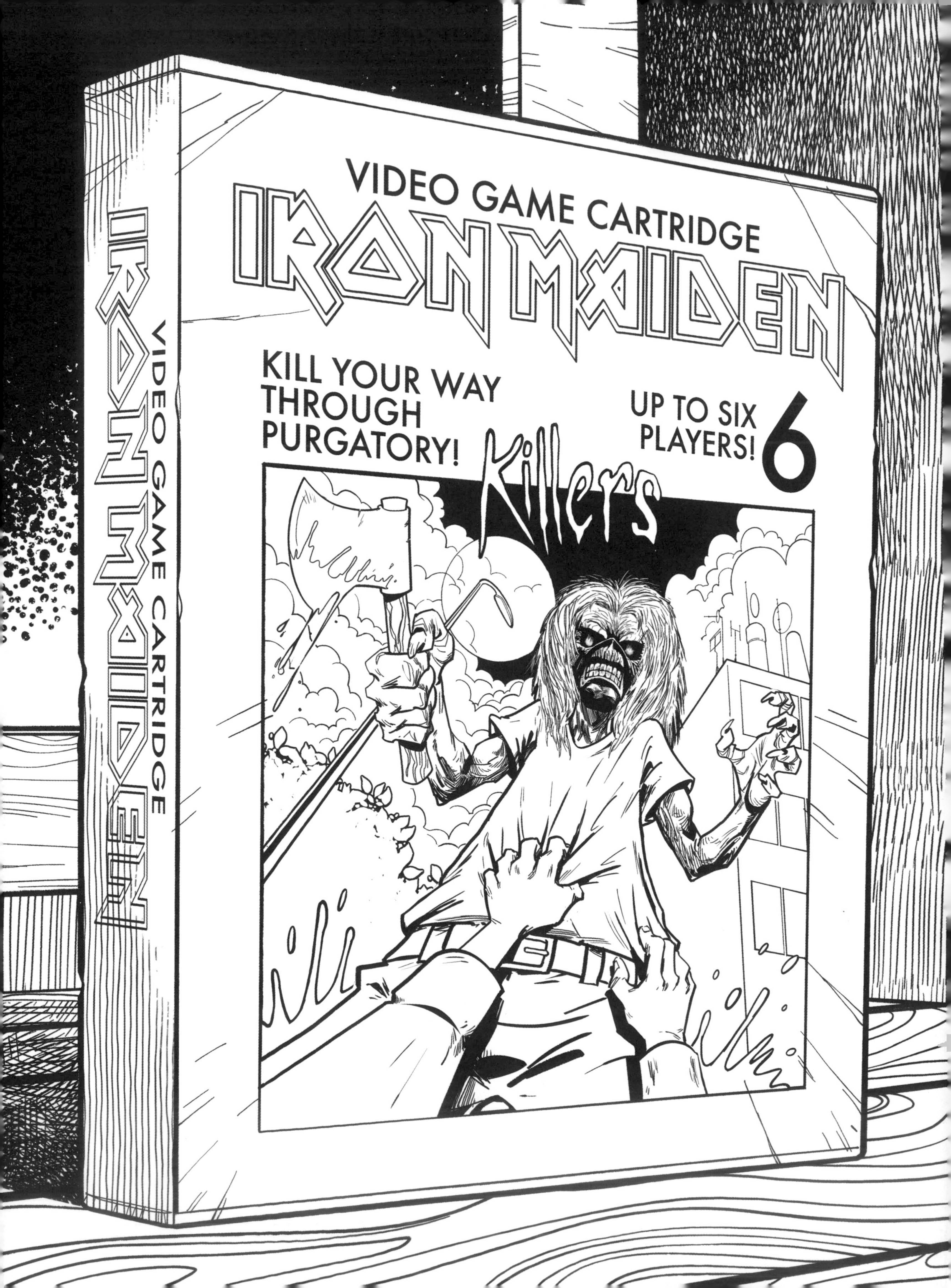
VIDEO GAME CARTRIDGE
IRON MAIDEN
KILL YOUR WAY THROUGH PURGATORY!
UP TO SIX PLAYERS!
6
Killers
VIDEO GAME CARTRIDGE
IRON MAIDEN

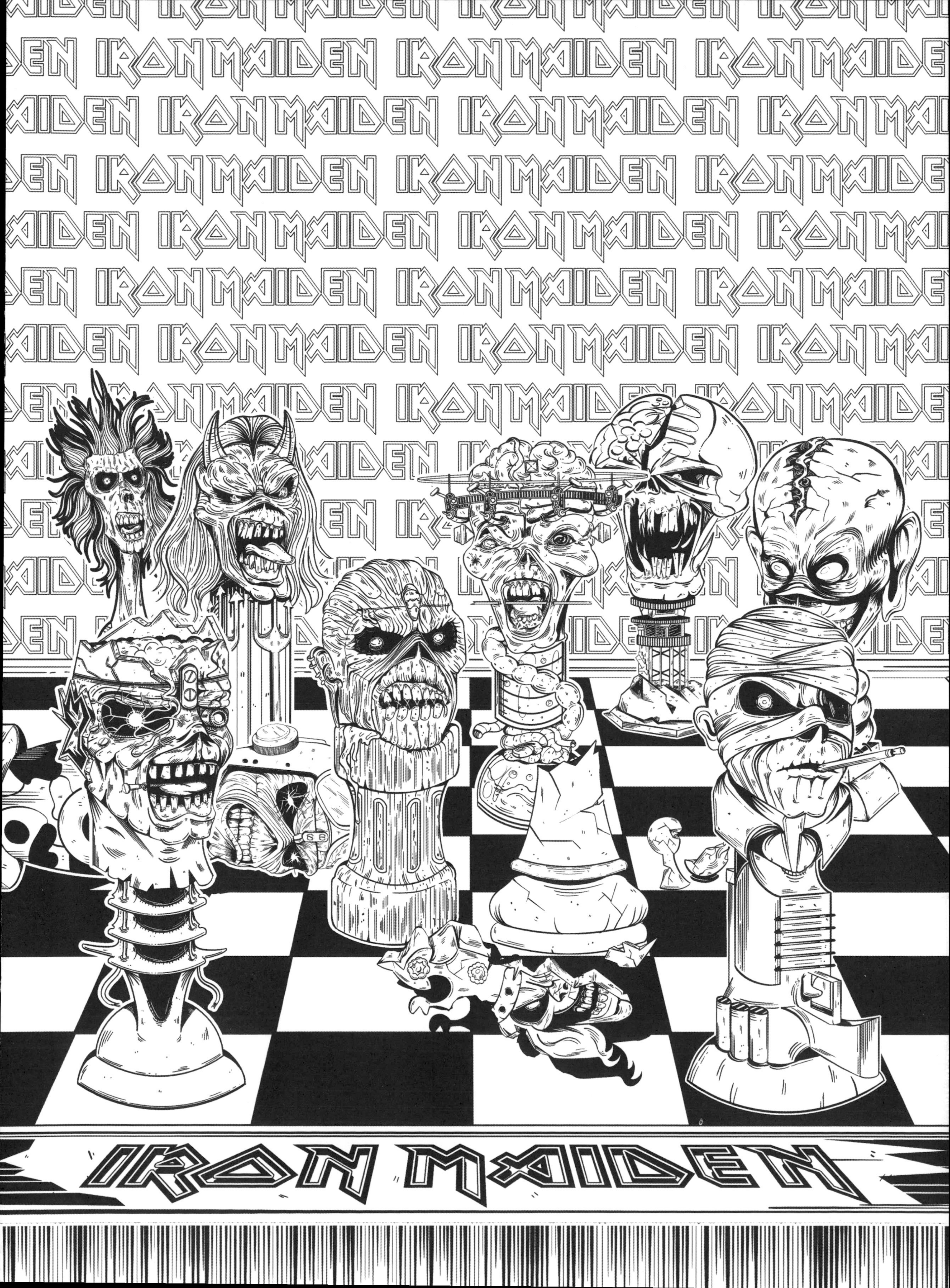
IRON MAIDEN

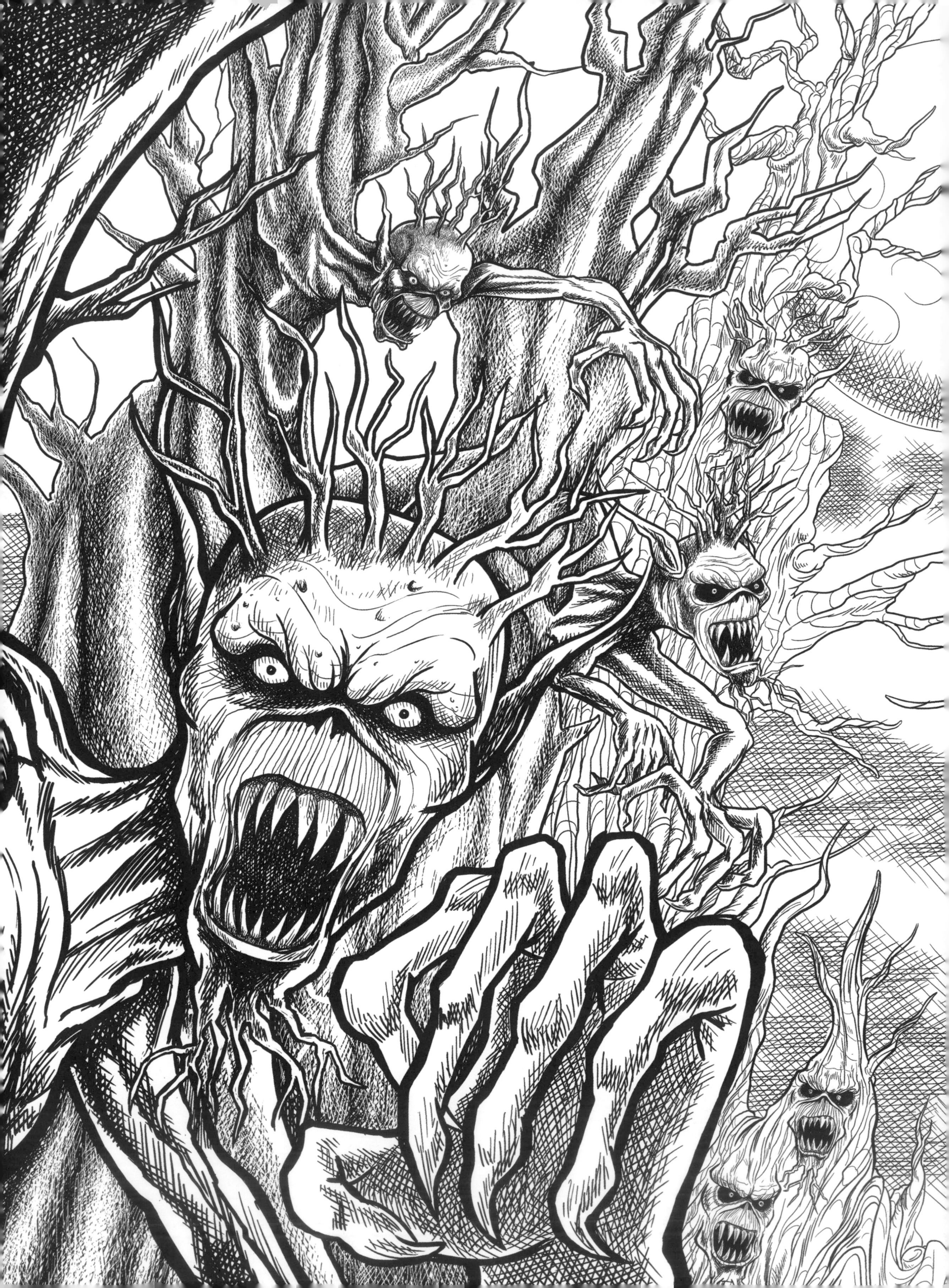

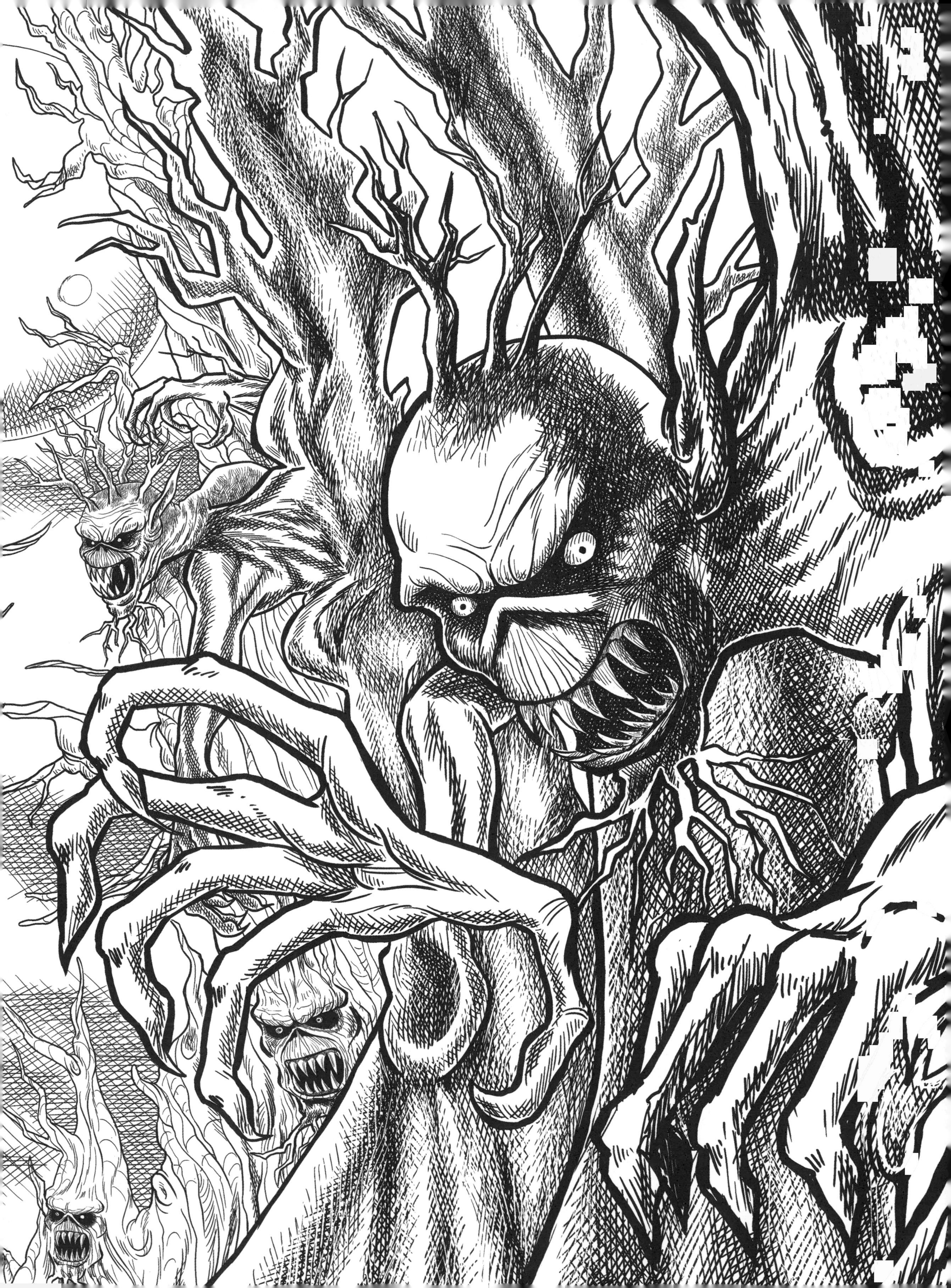

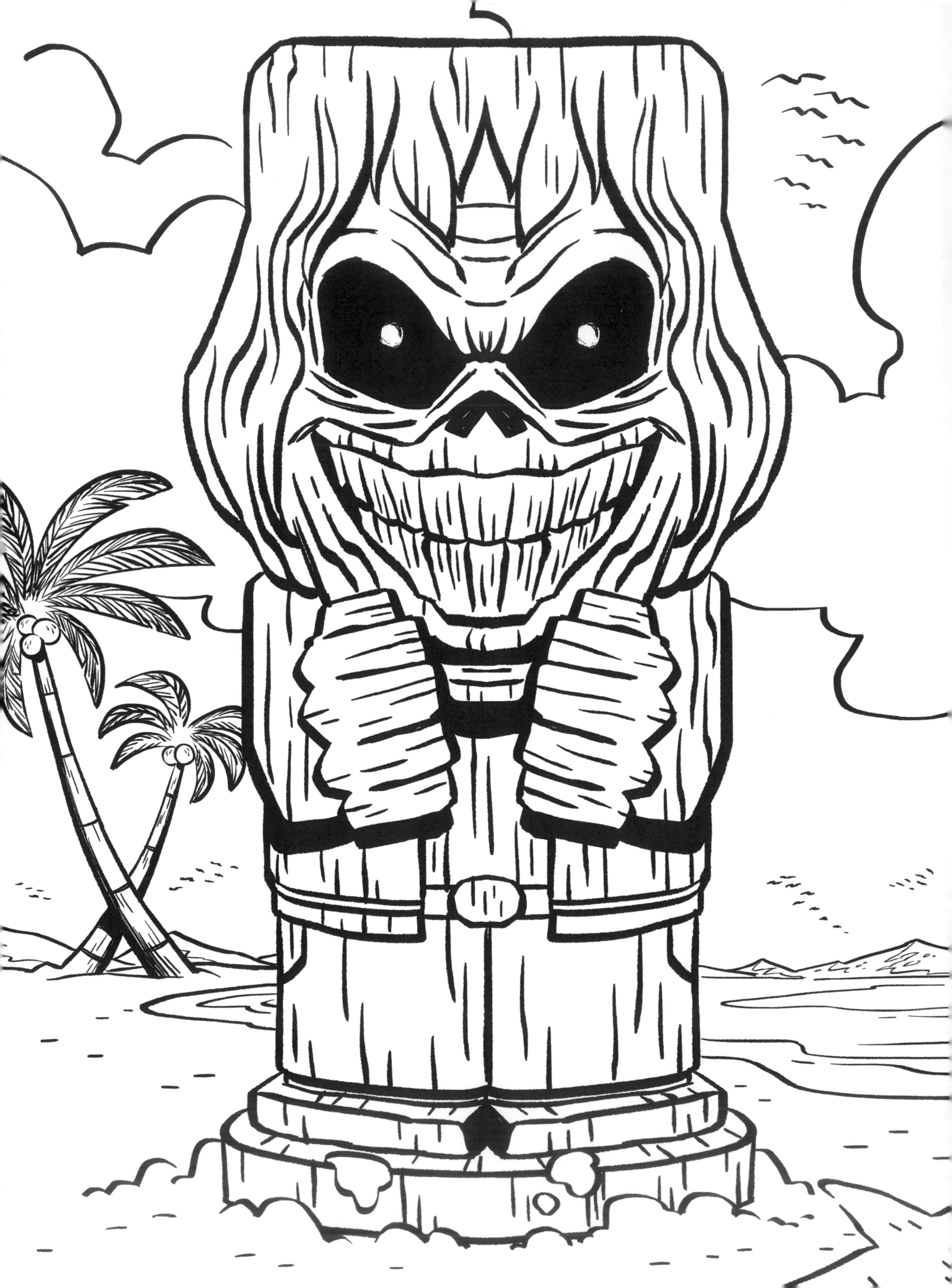

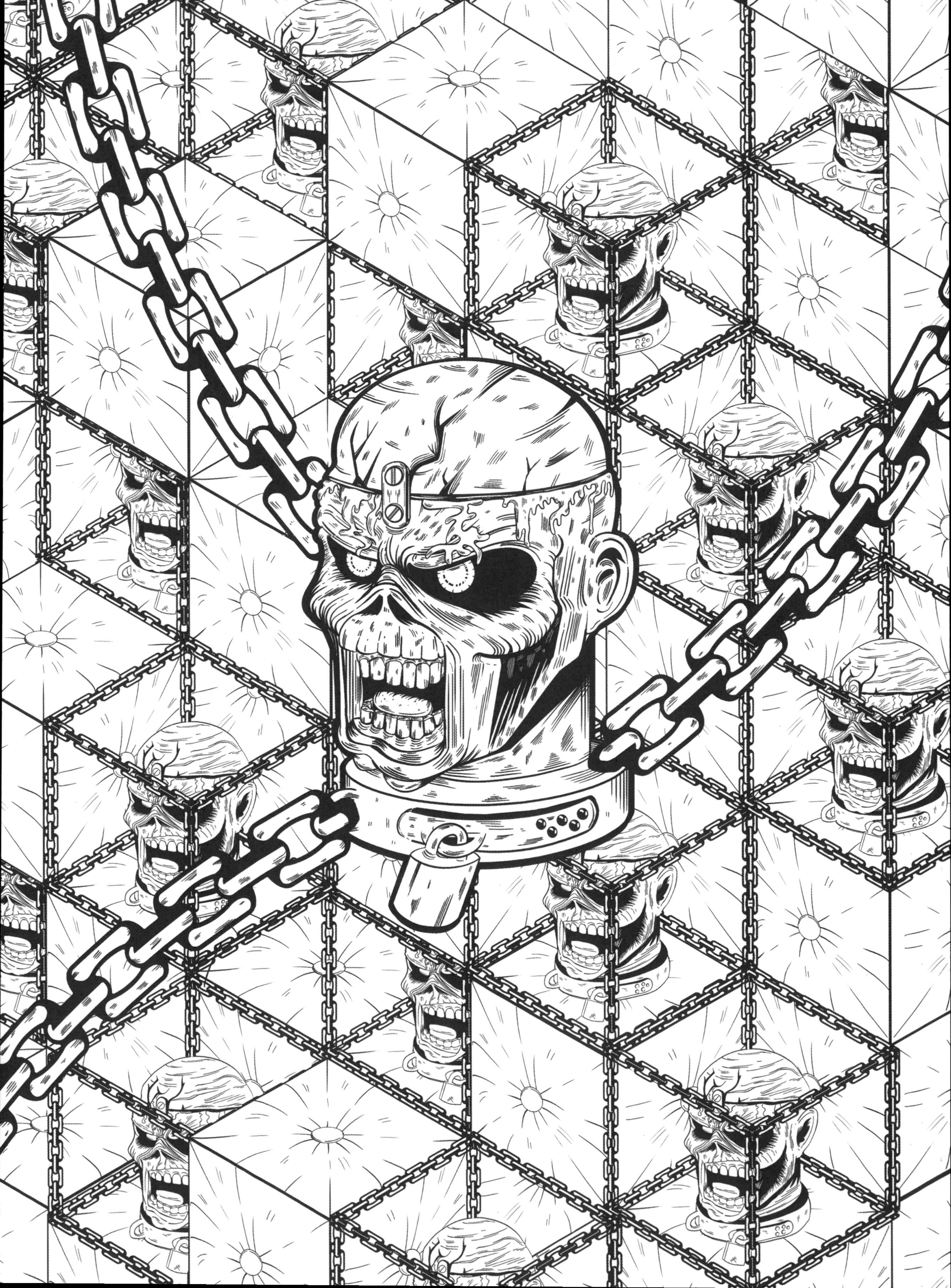

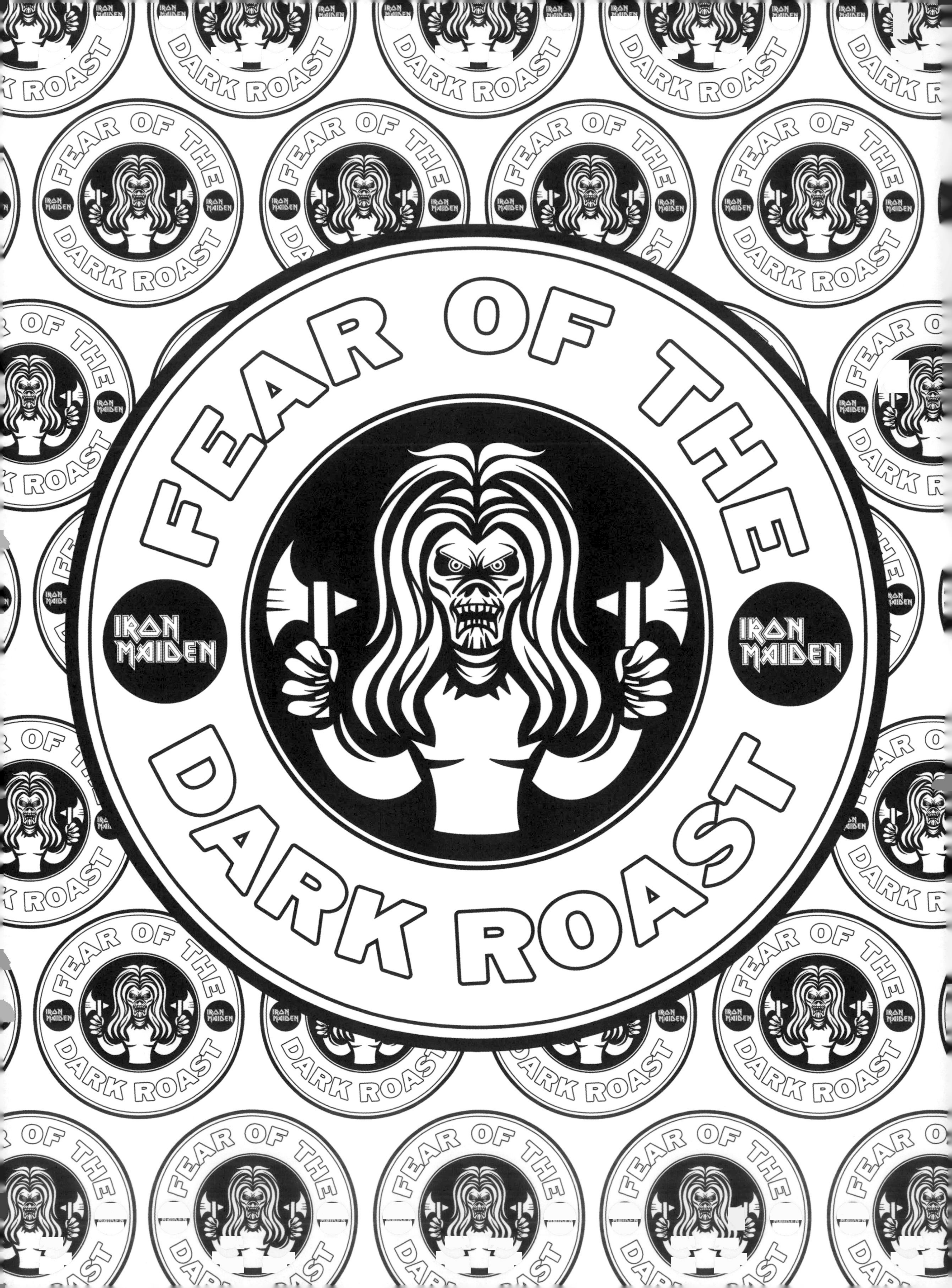
FEAR OF THE
IRON MAIDEN
IRON MAIDEN
DARK ROAST

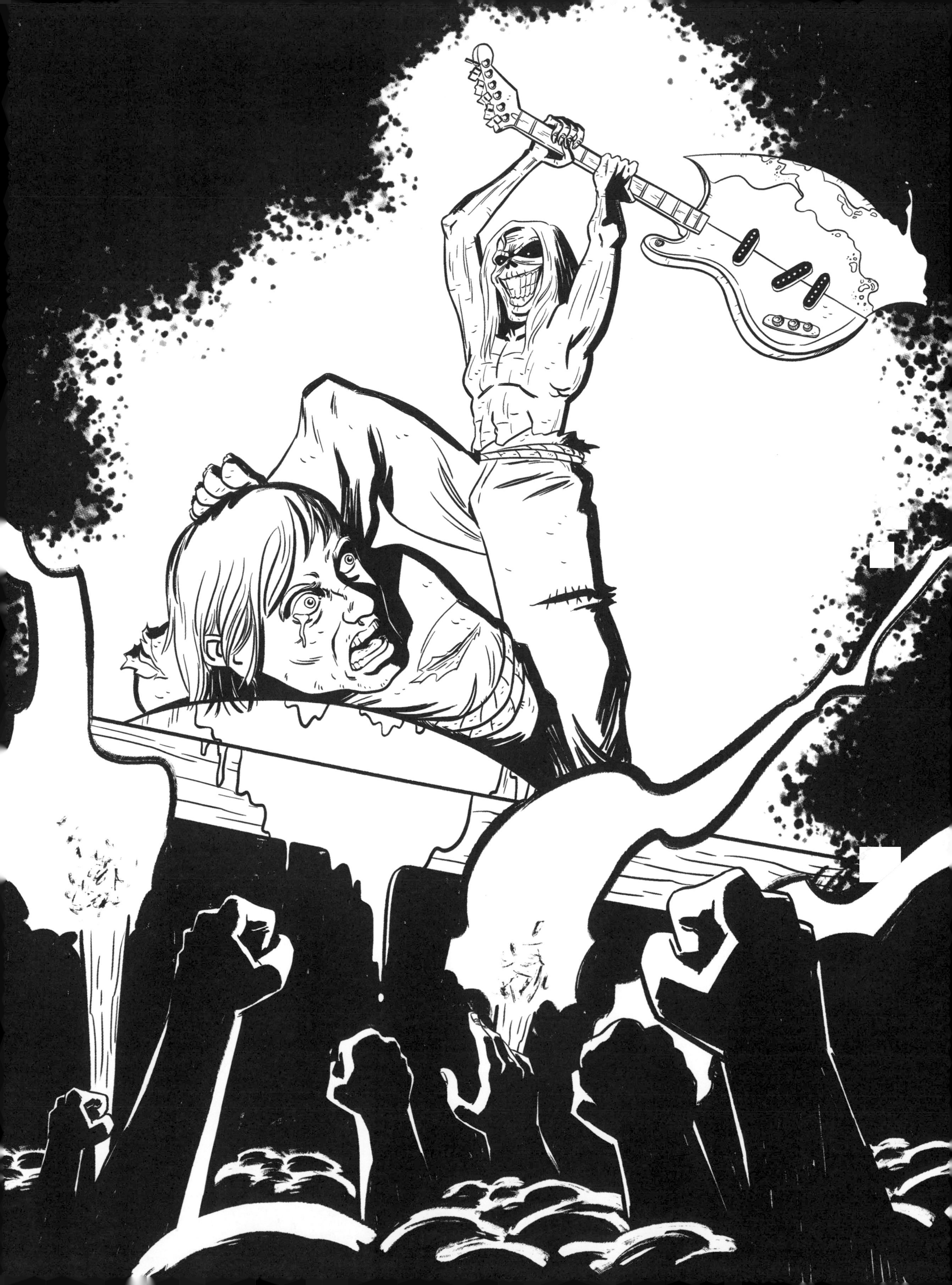

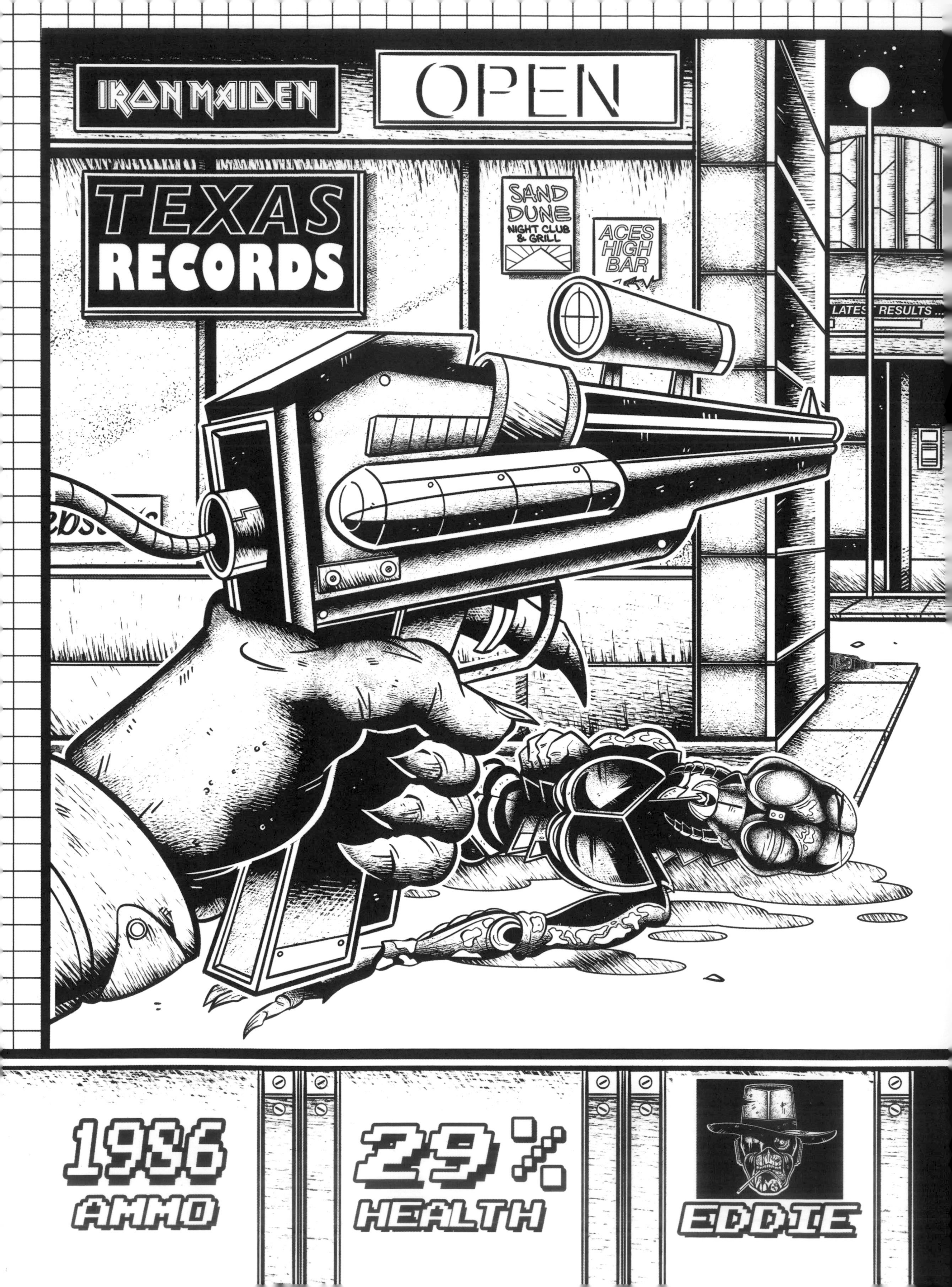
IRON MAIDEN
OPEN
TEXAS
RECORDS
SAND DUNE
NIGHT CLUB & GRILL
ACES HIGH BAR
LATEST RESULTS ...
1986
AMMO
29%
HEALTH
EDDIE

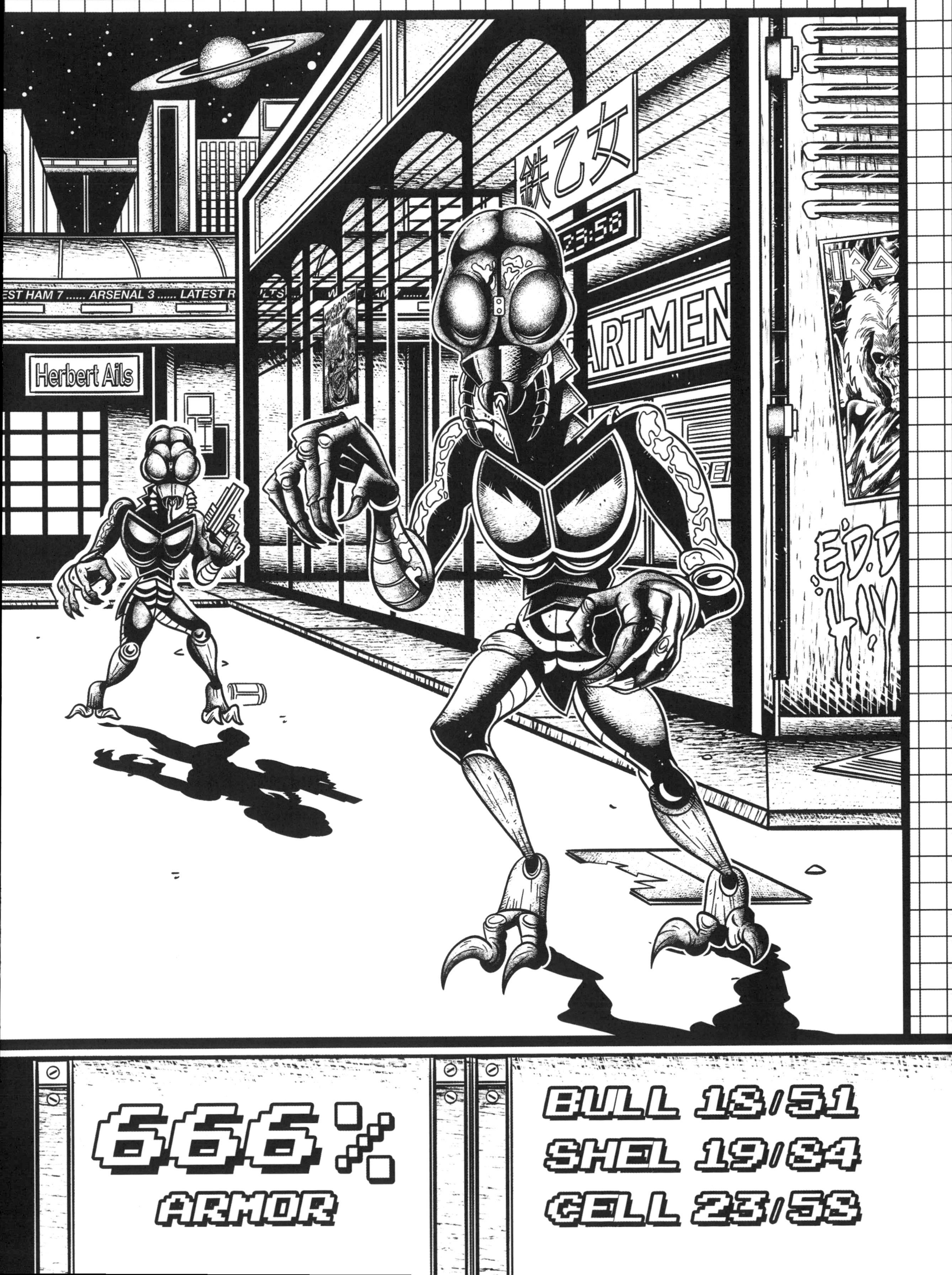
EST HAM 7 ...... ARSENAL 3 ...... LATEST R
Herbert Ails
鉄乙女
23:58
666%
ARMOR
BULL 18/51
SHEL 19/84
CELL 23/58

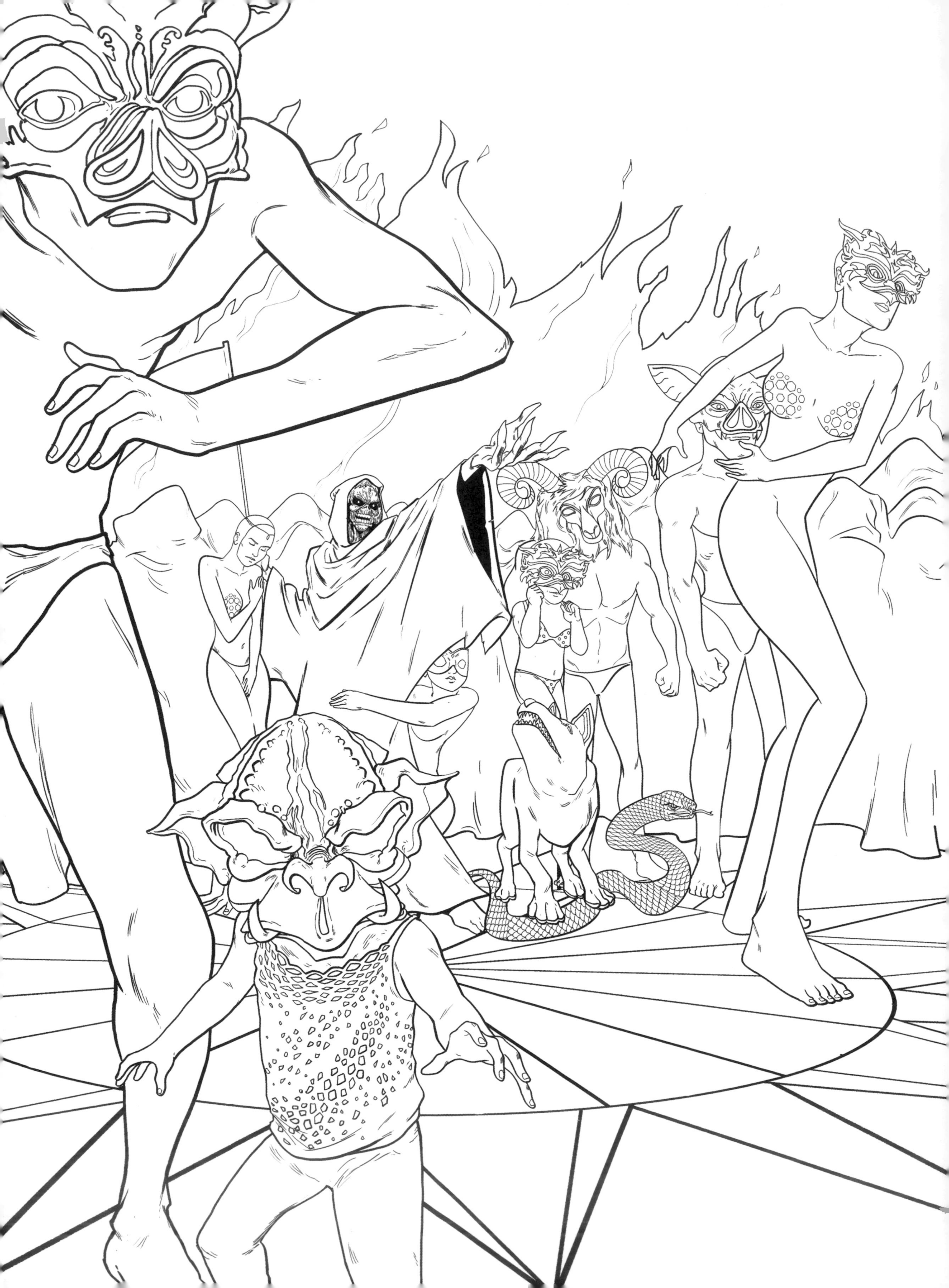

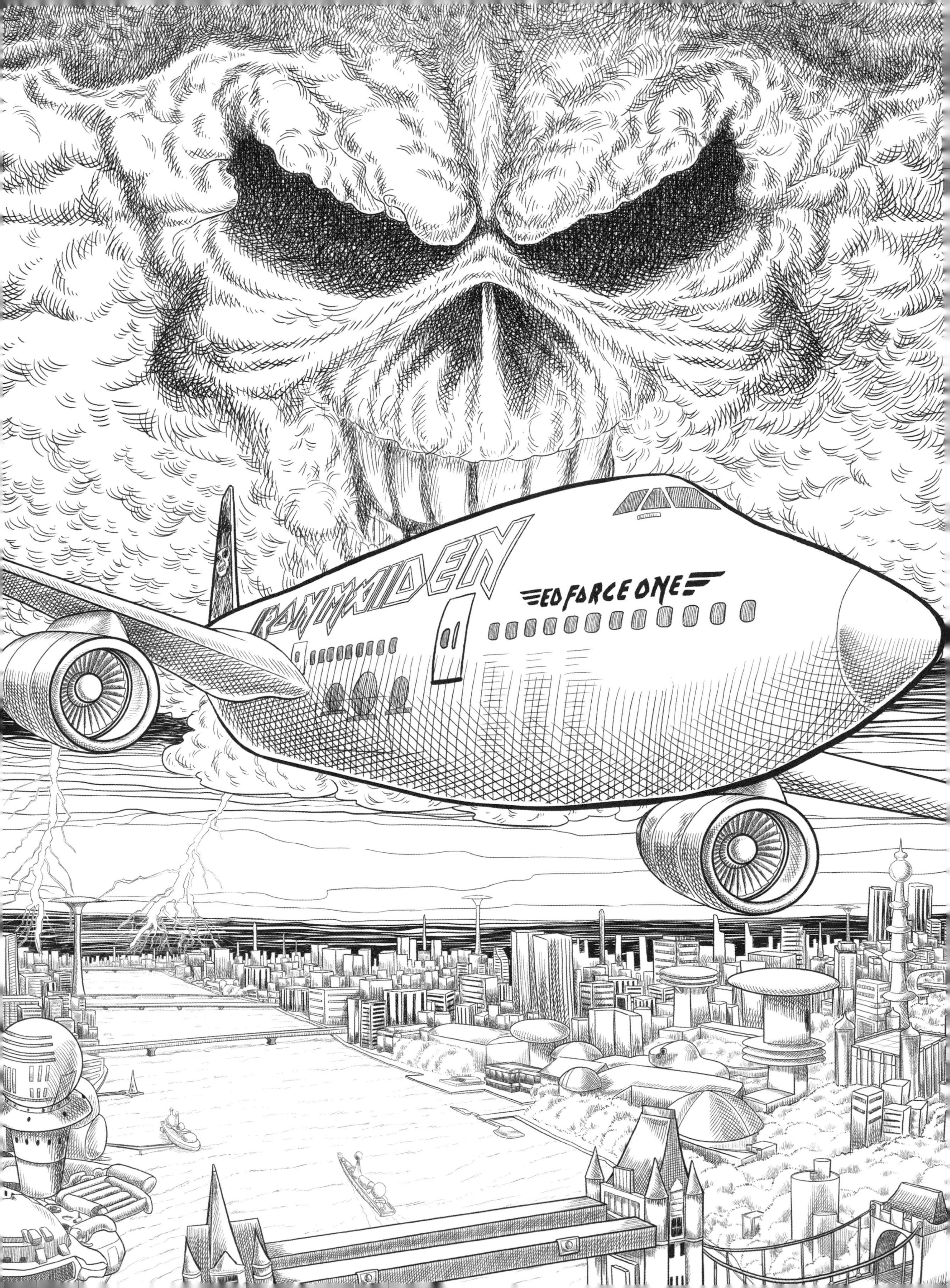
IRON MAIDEN
ED FORCE ONE

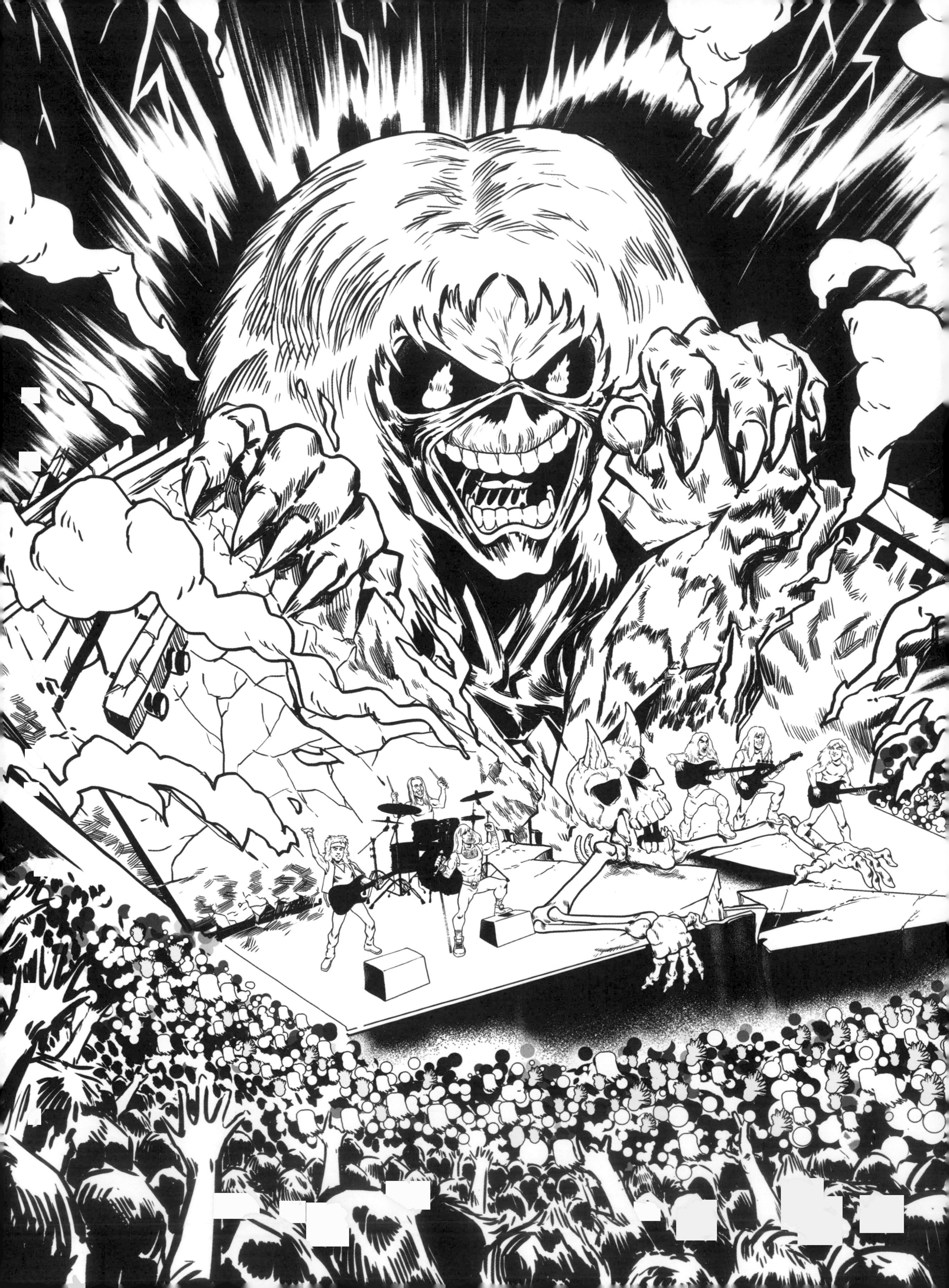

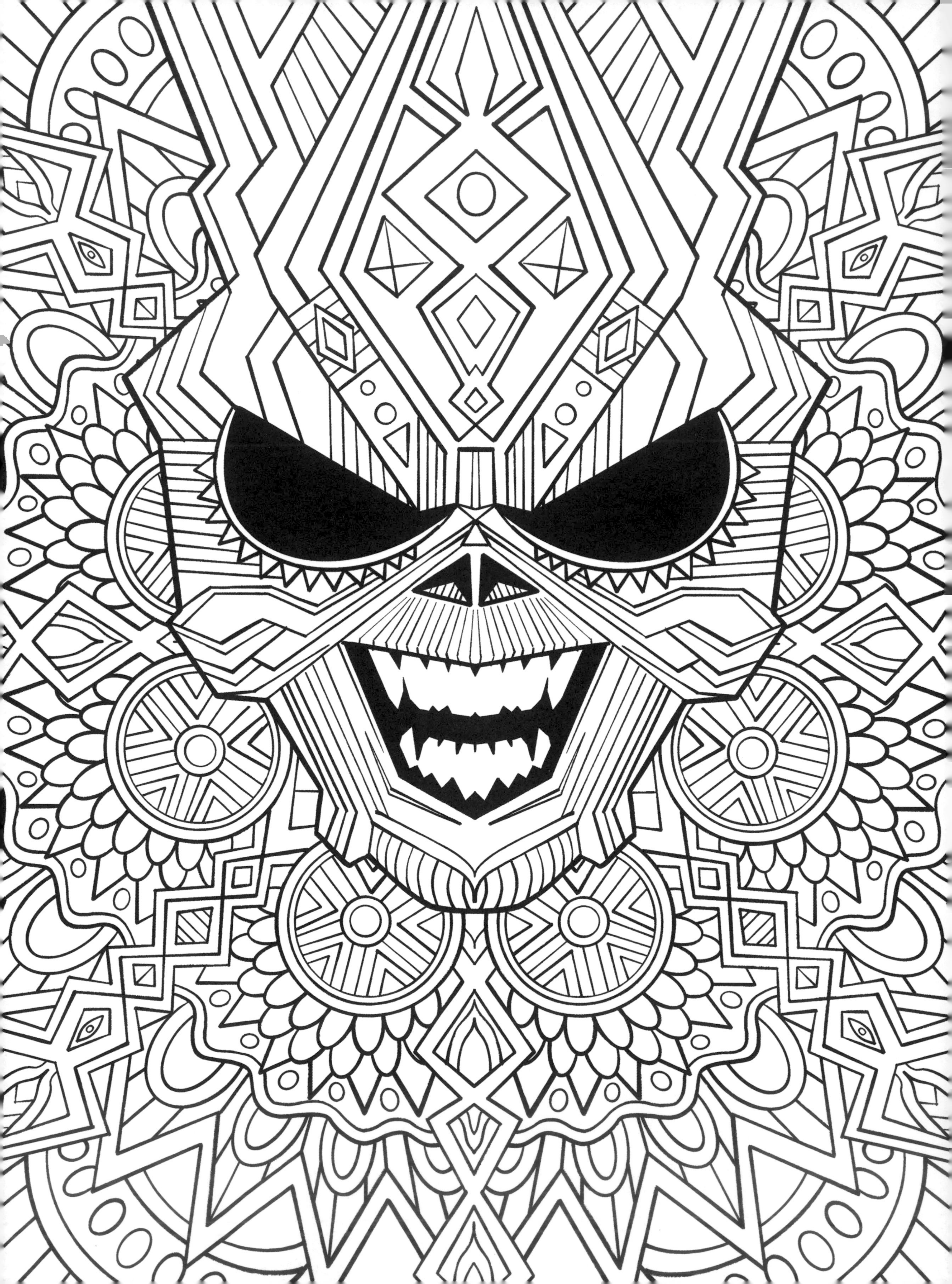

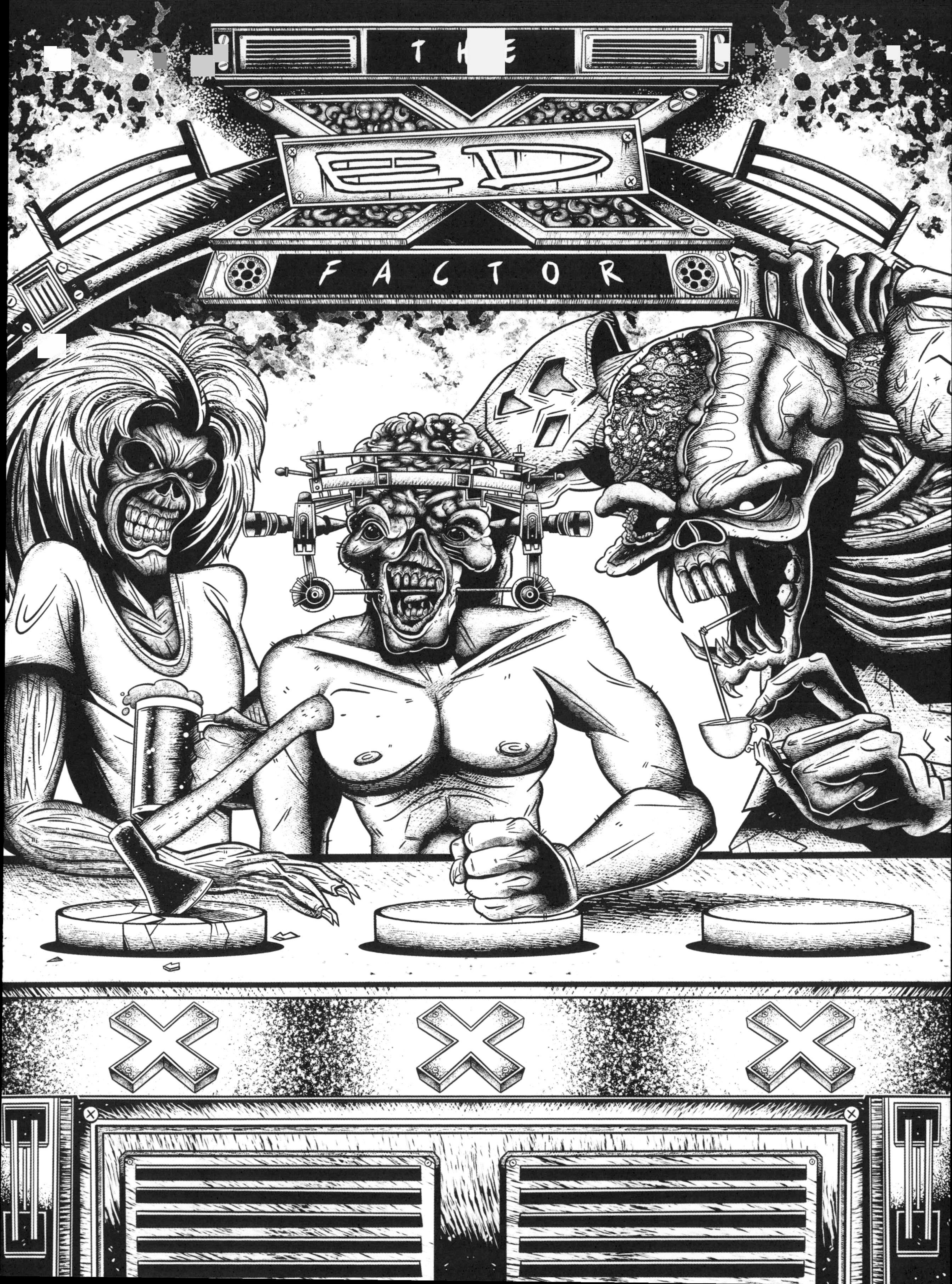
THE
ED
FACTOR

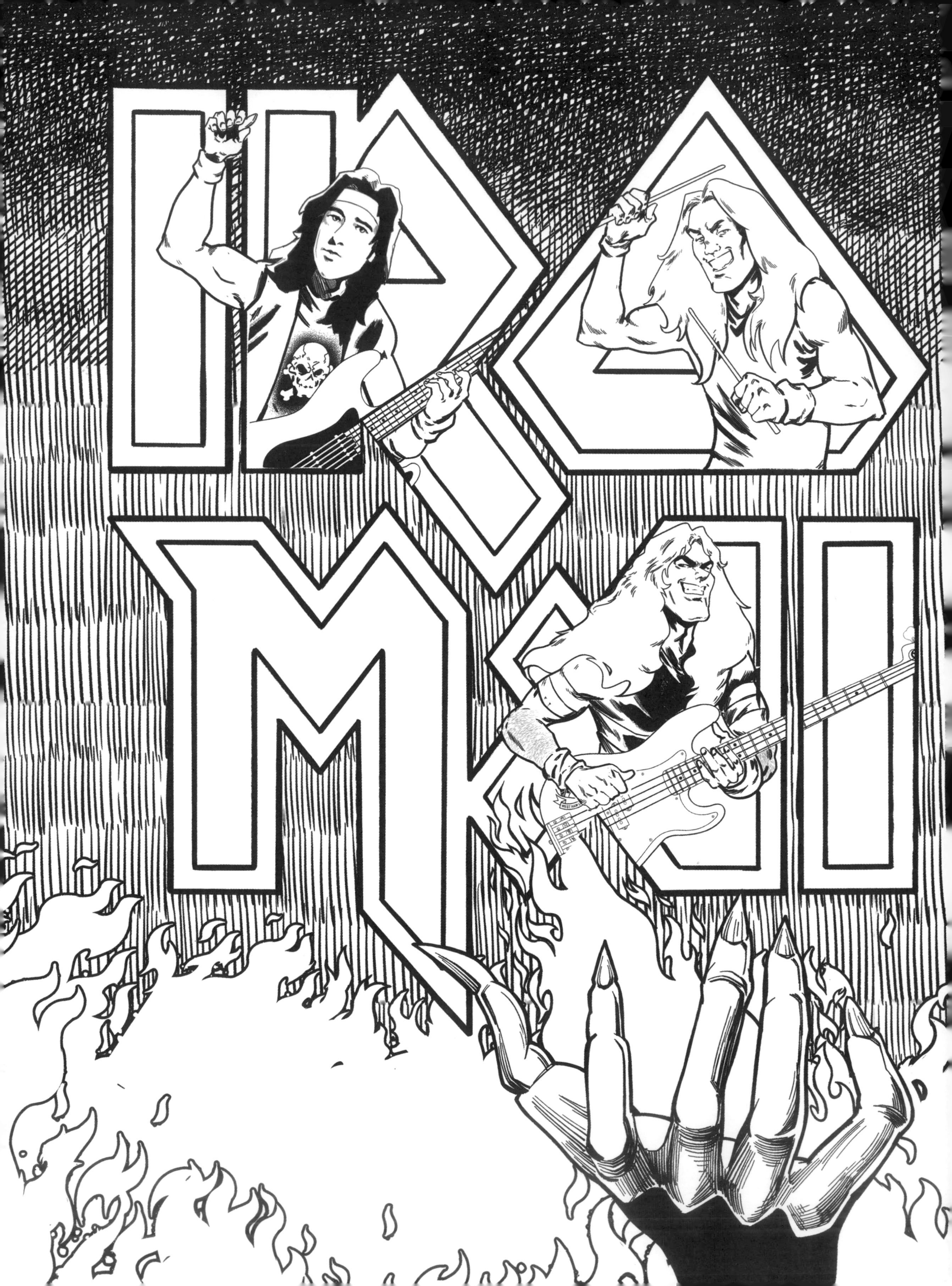

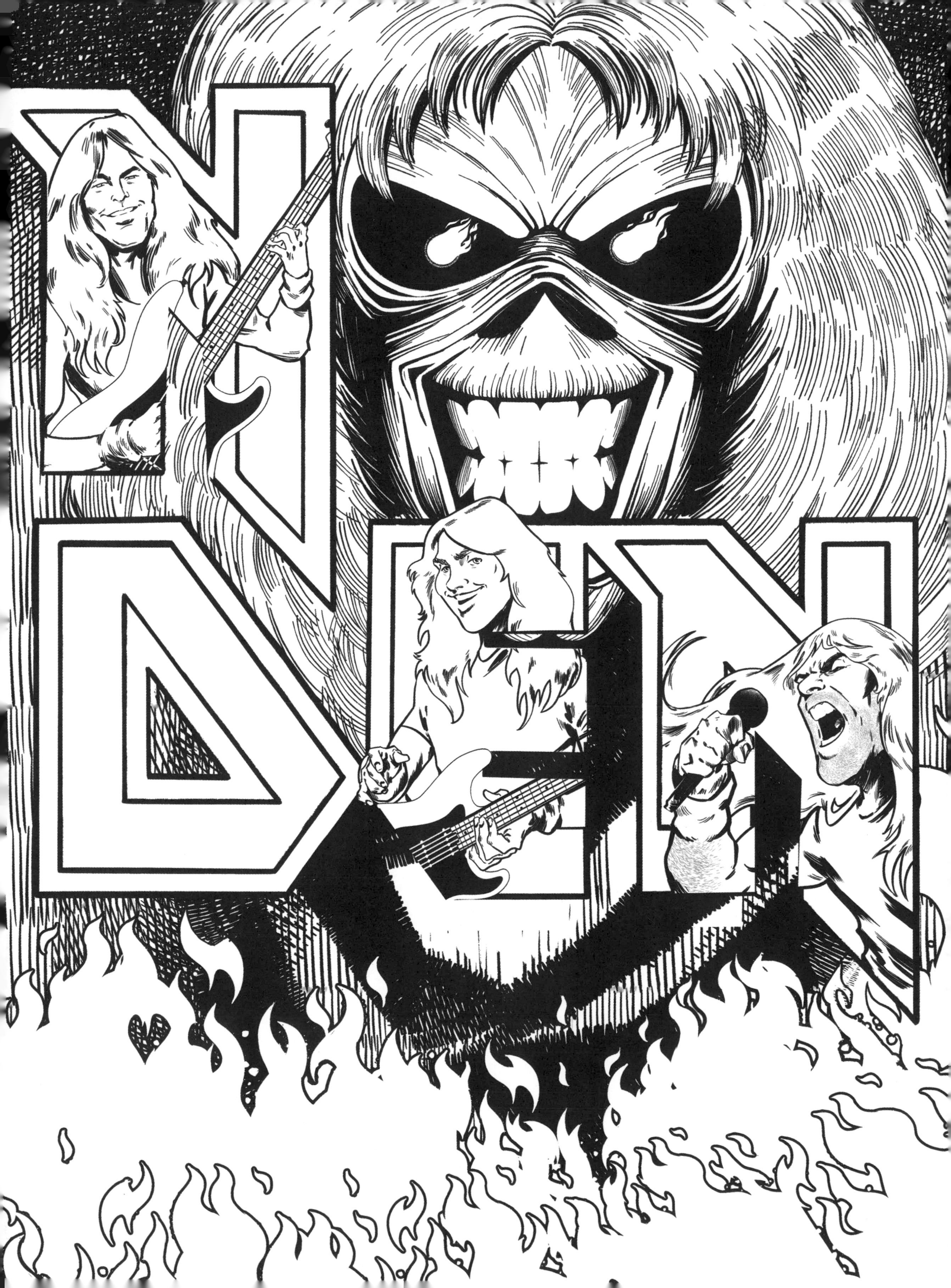

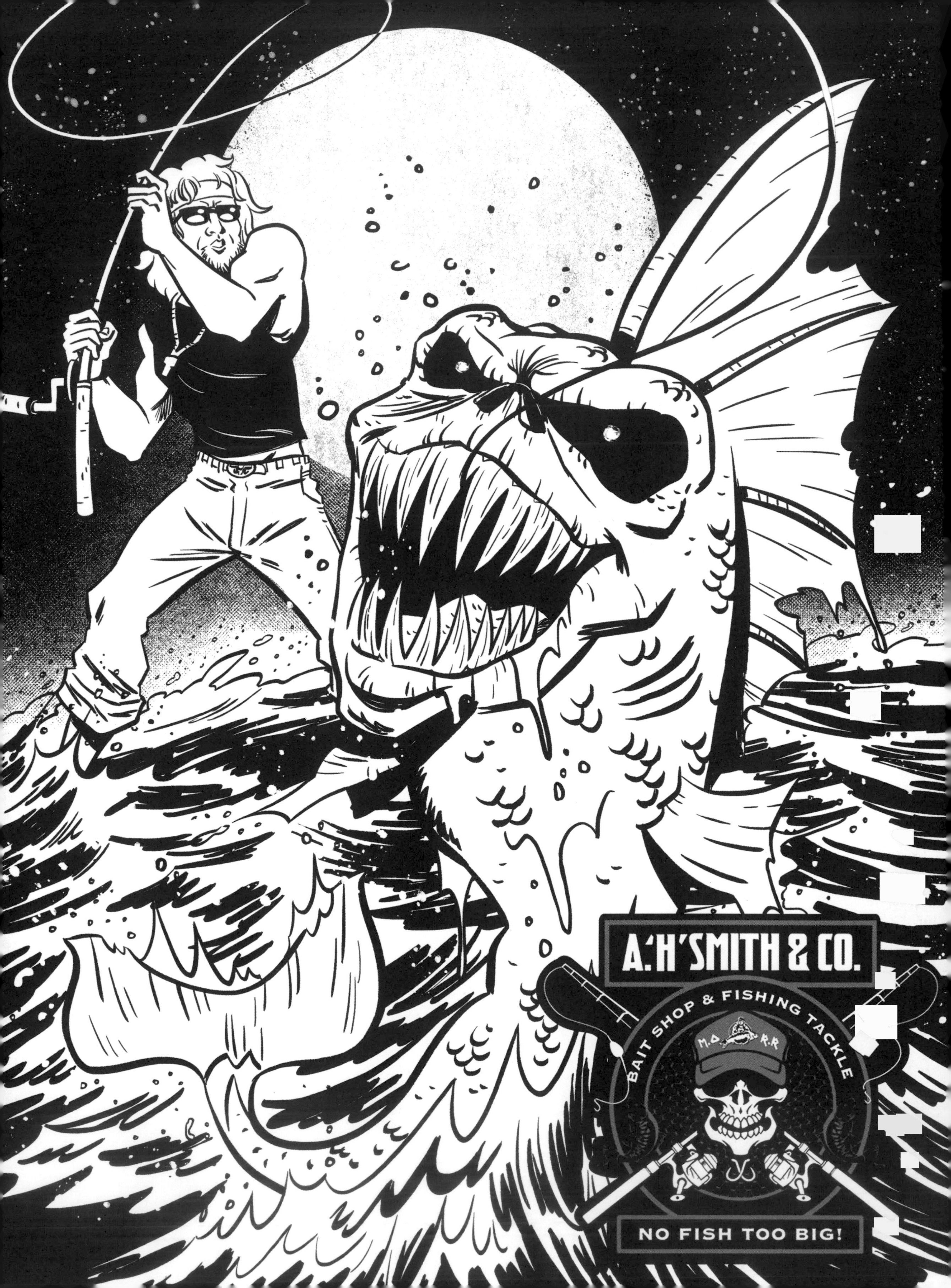
A.'H'SMITH & CO.
BAIT SHOP & FISHING TACKLE
NO FISH TOO BIG!

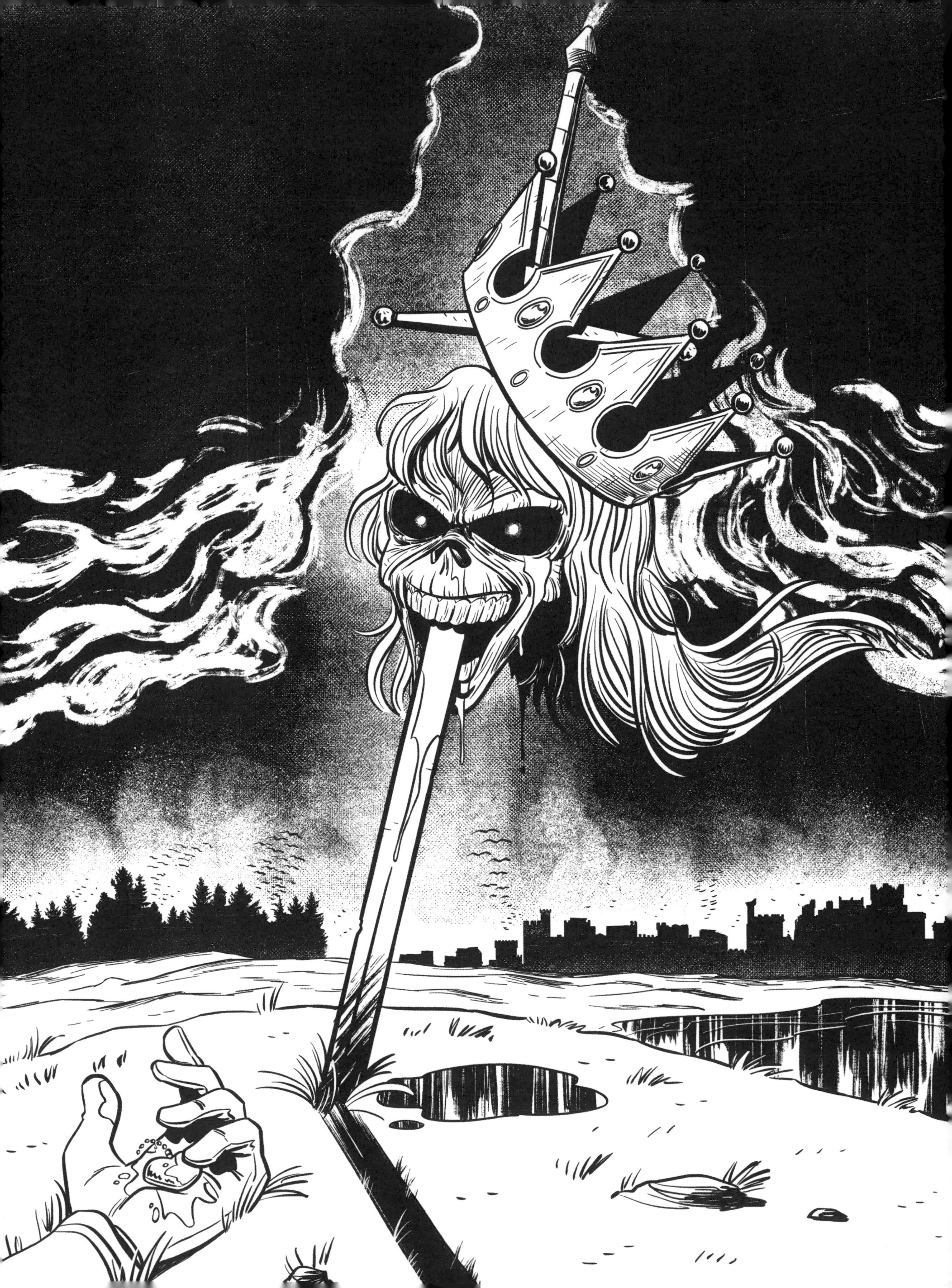

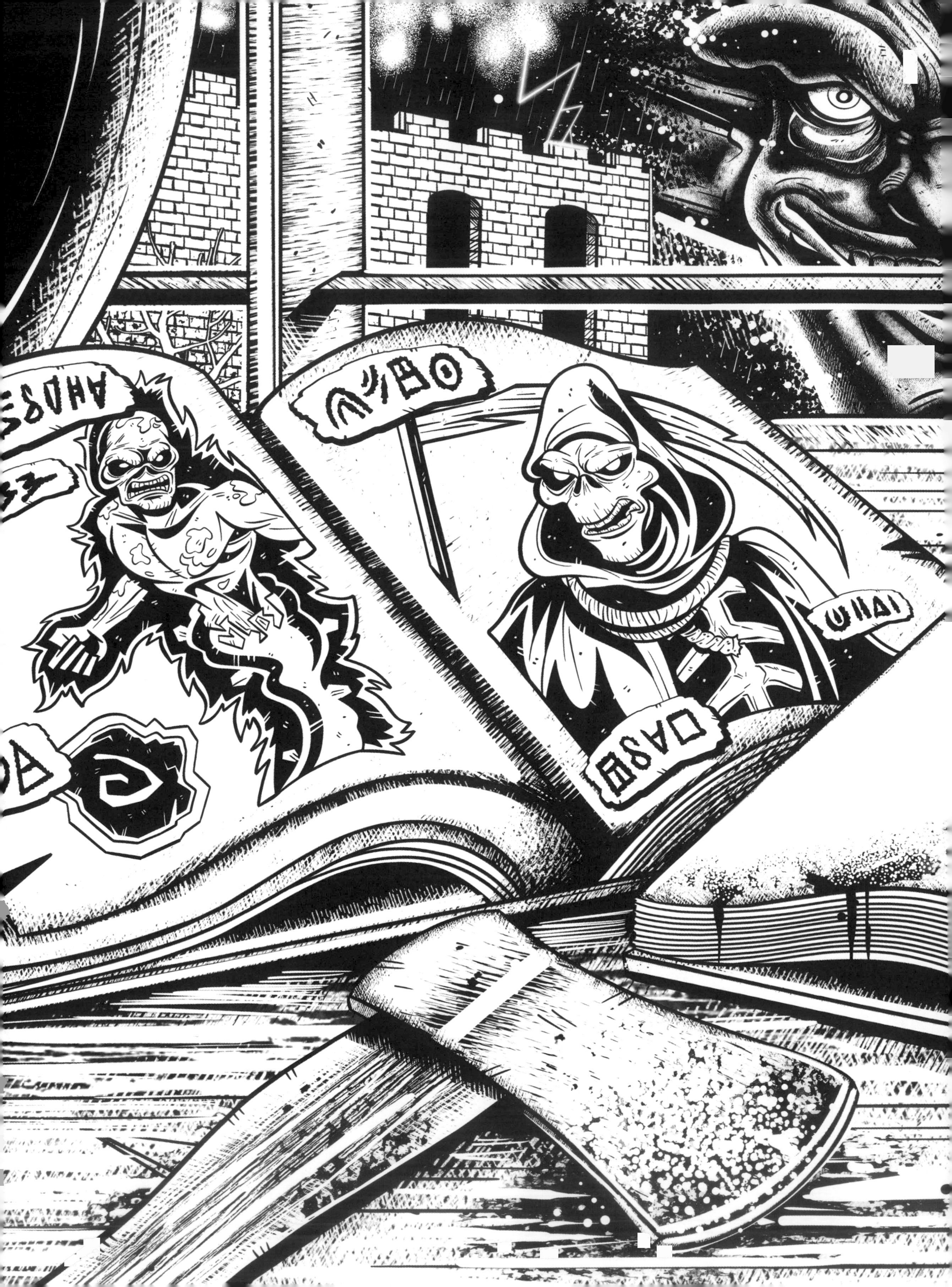

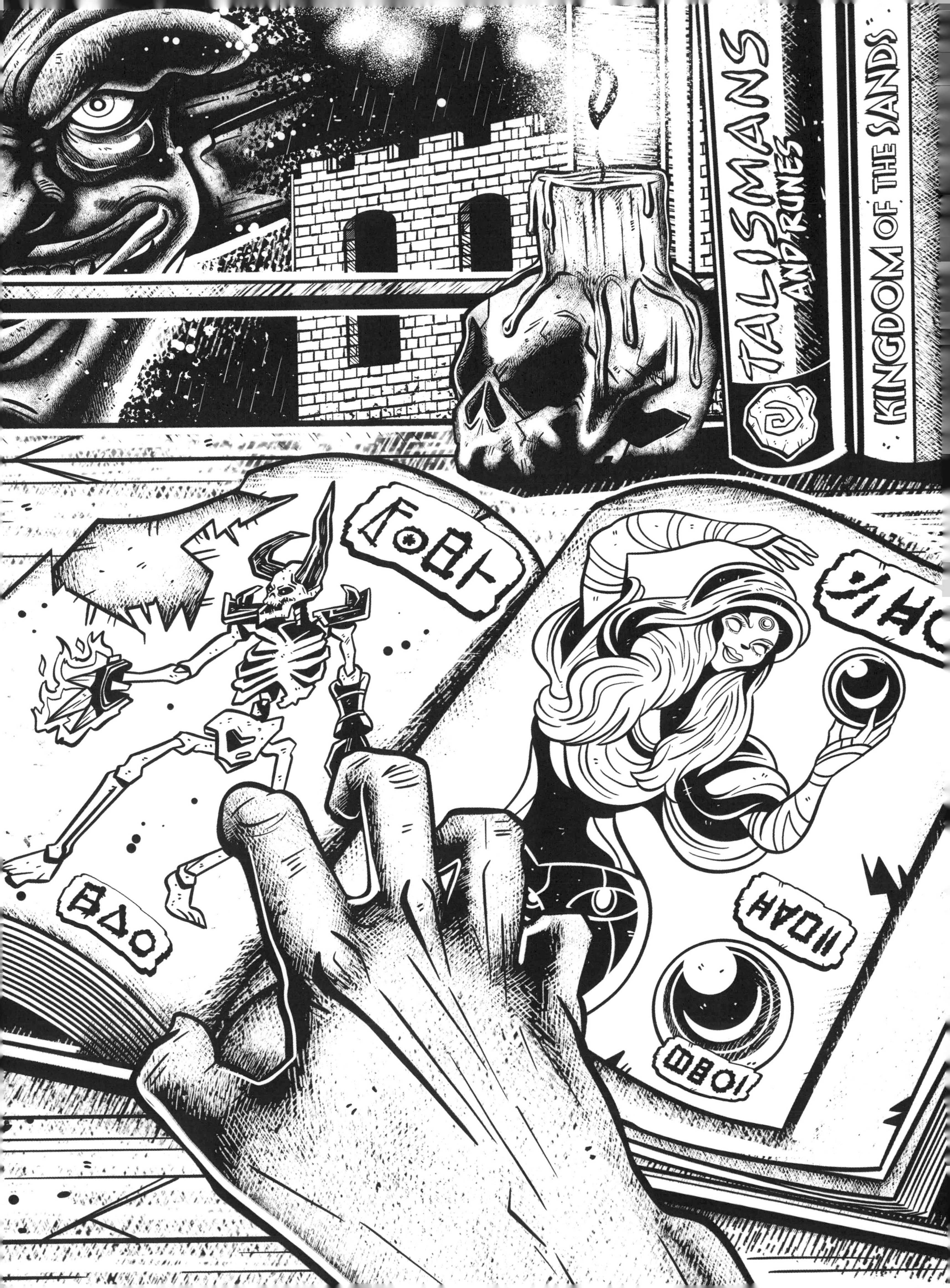
TALISMANS AND RUNES
KINGDOM OF THE SANDS

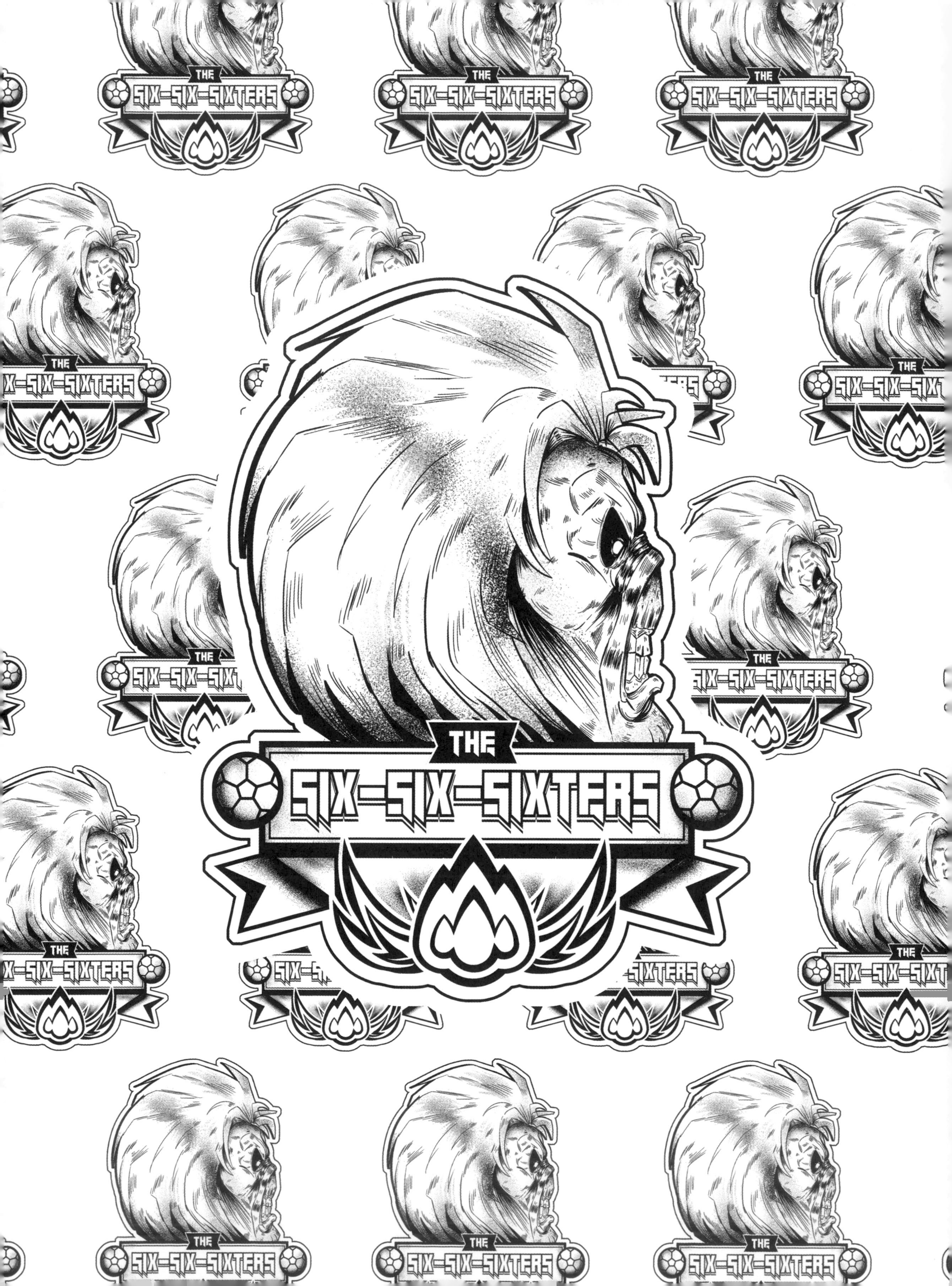
THE
SIX-SIX-SIXTERS

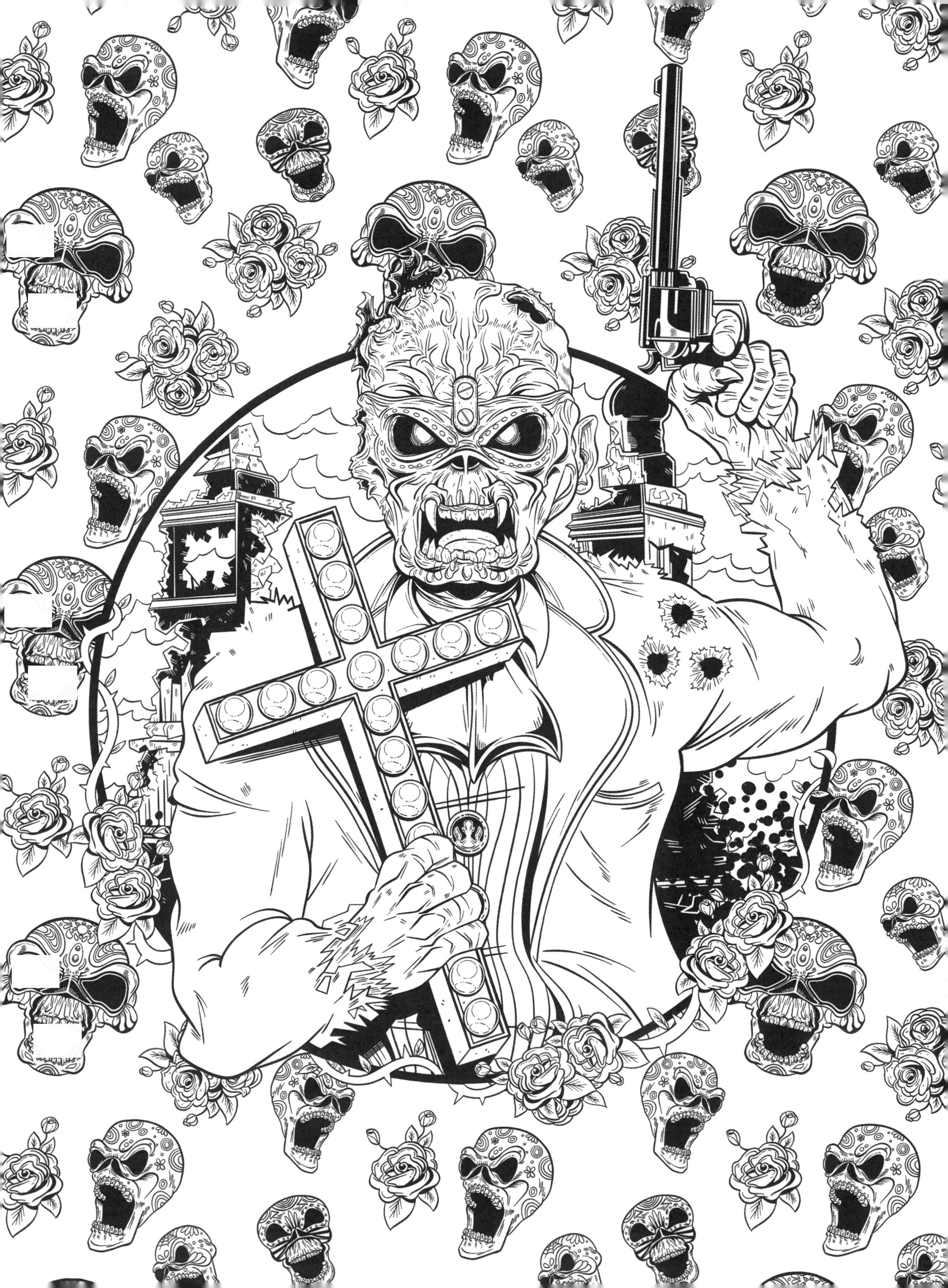

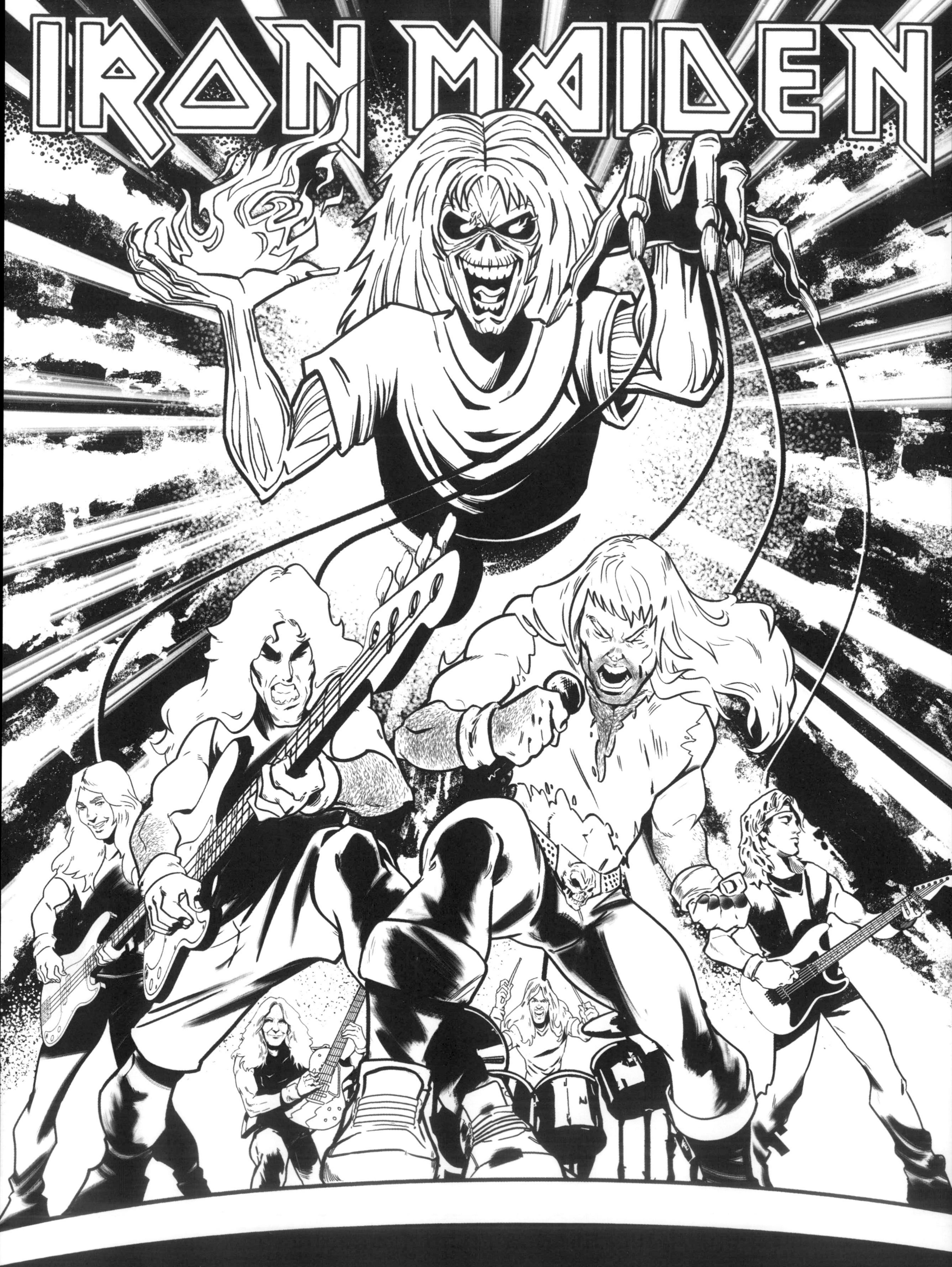
IRON MAIDEN

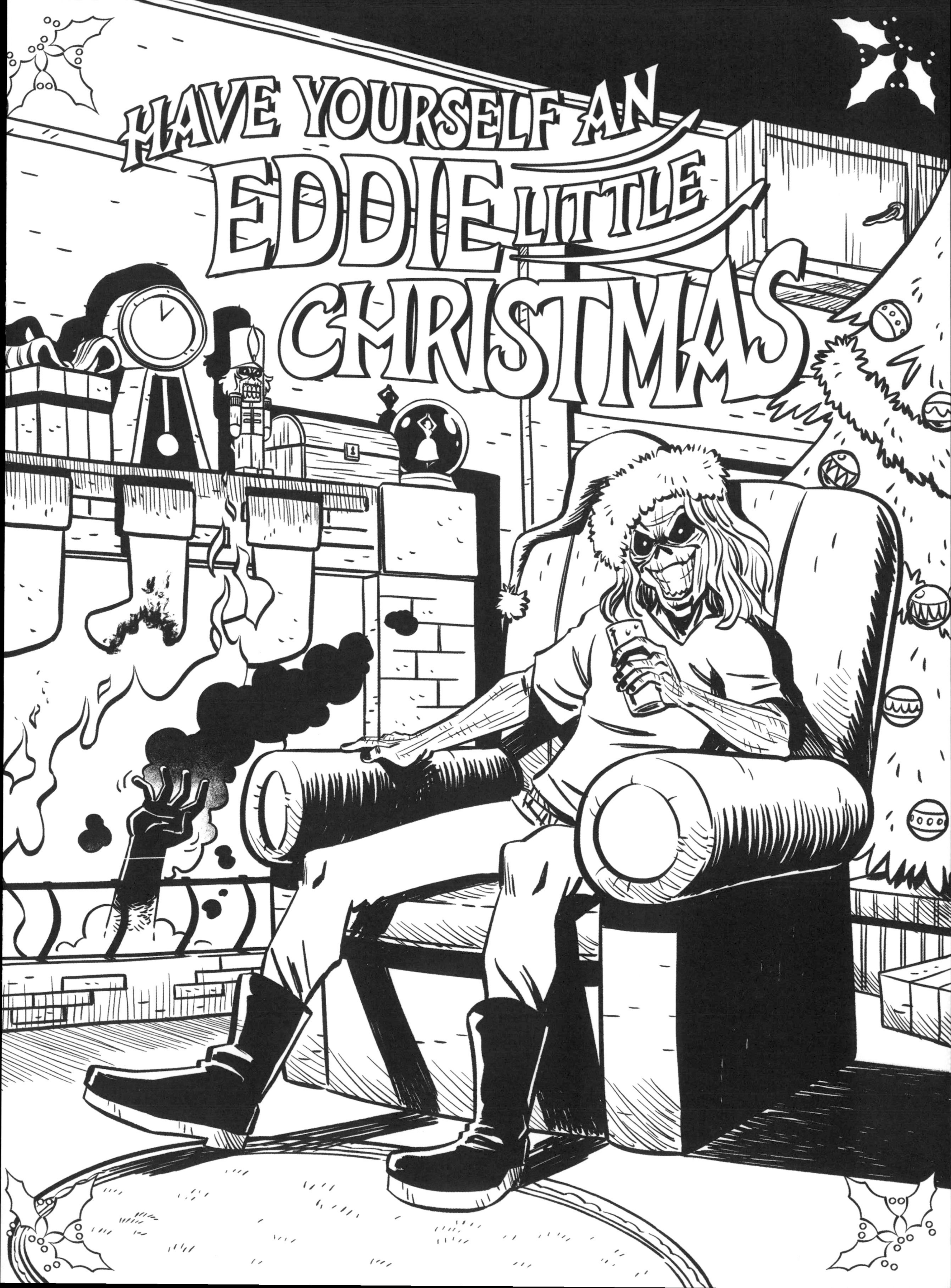
HAVE YOURSELF AN
EDDIE LITTLE
CHRISTMAS

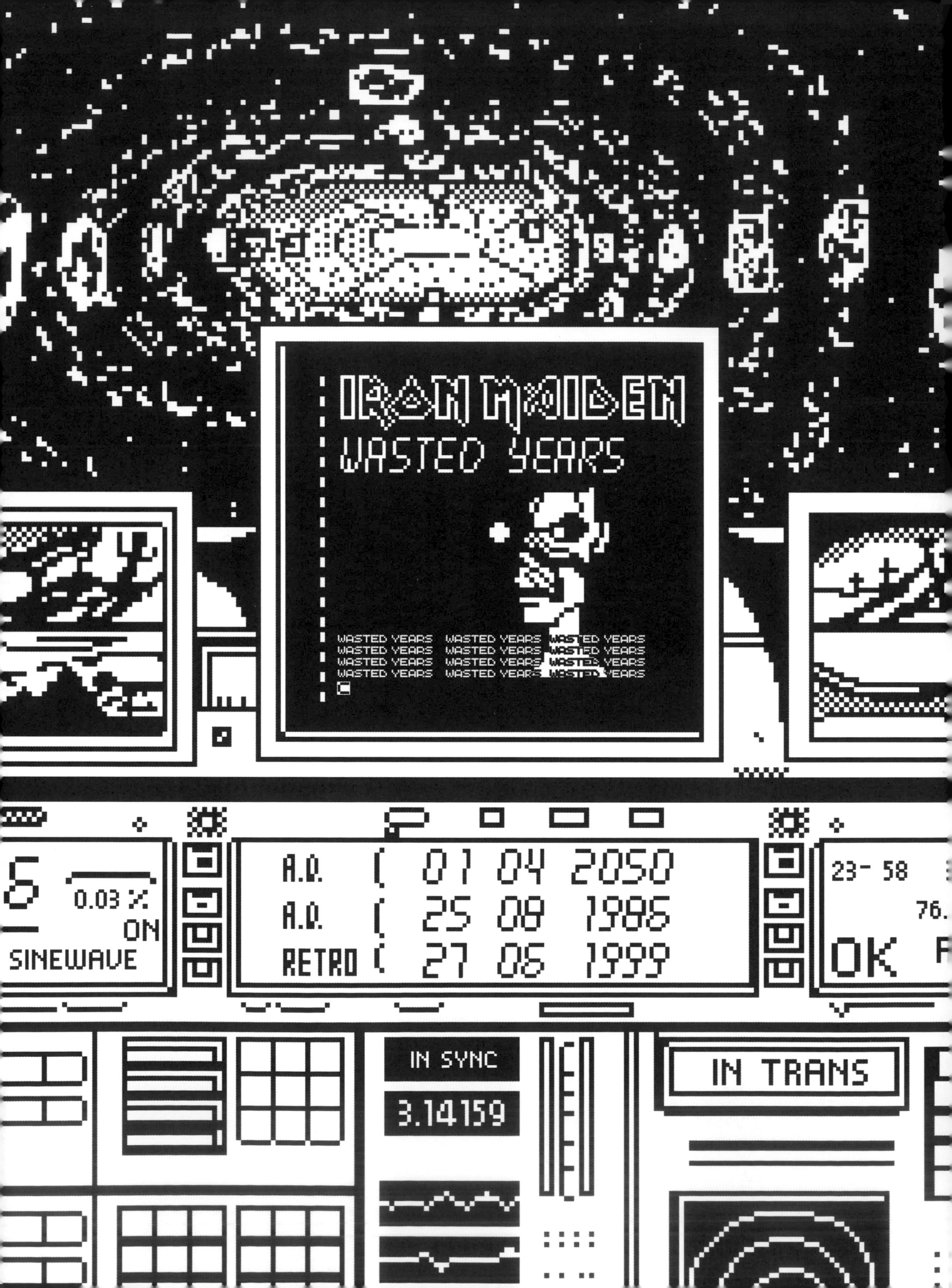

IRON MAIDEN
WASTED YEARS
WASTED YEARS WASTED YEARS WASTED YEARS
WASTED YEARS WASTED YEARS WASTED YEARS
WASTED YEARS WASTED YEARS WASTED YEARS
WASTED YEARS WASTED YEARS WASTED YEARS
0.03 %
ON
SINEWAVE
A.D. 01 04 2050
A.D. 25 08 1986
RETRO 27 05 1999
23- 58
OK
IN SYNC
3.14159
IN TRANS

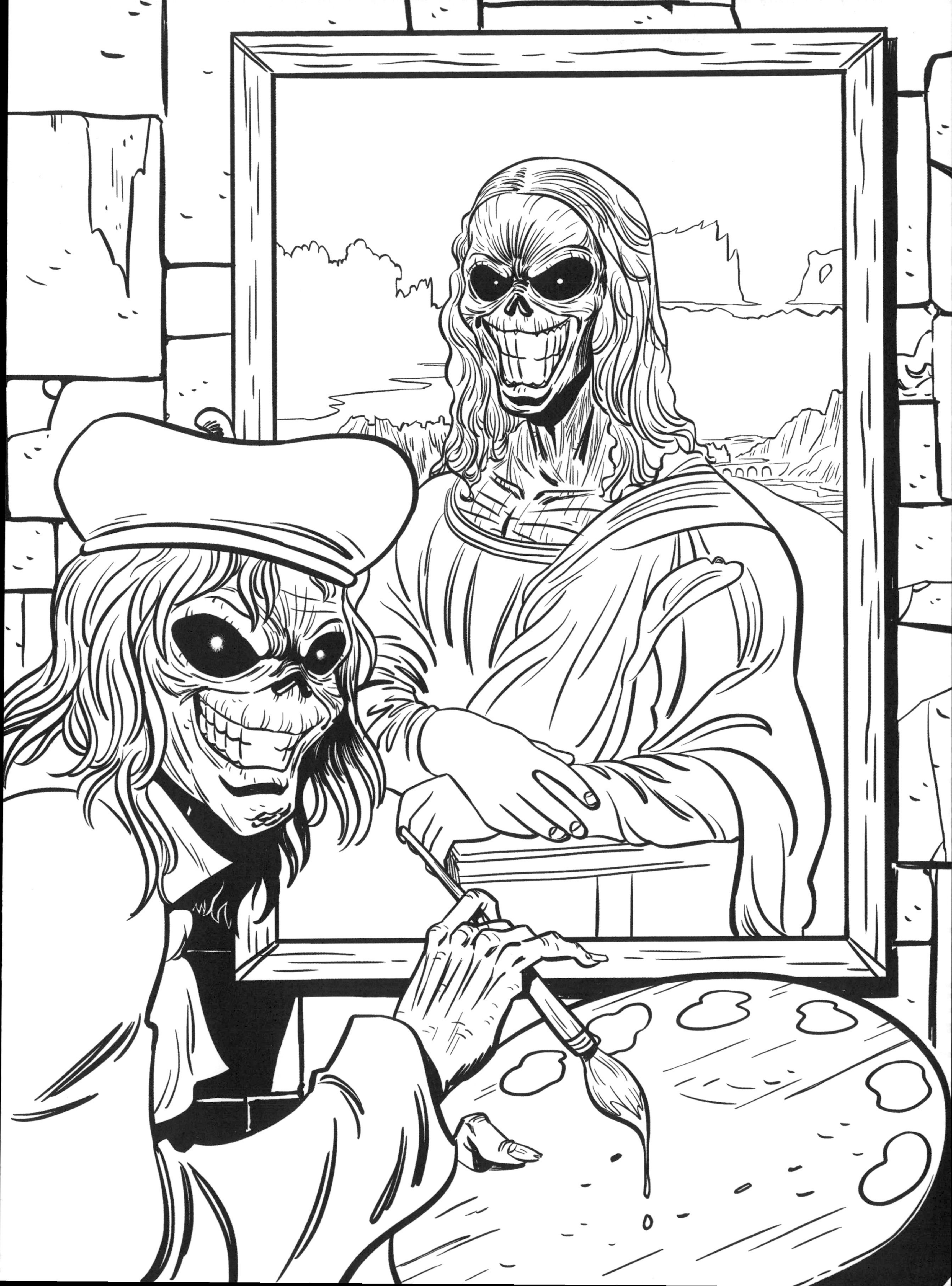

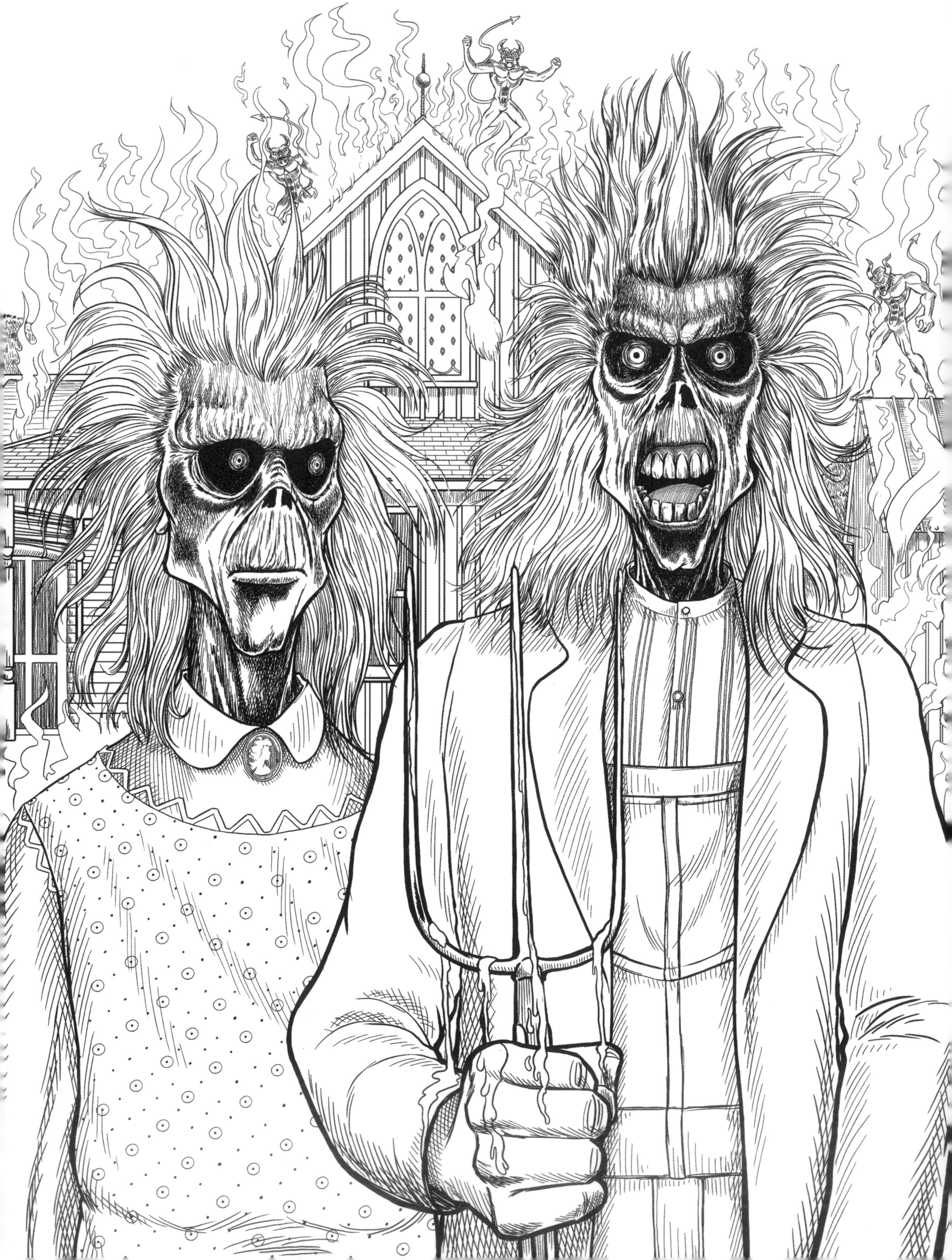

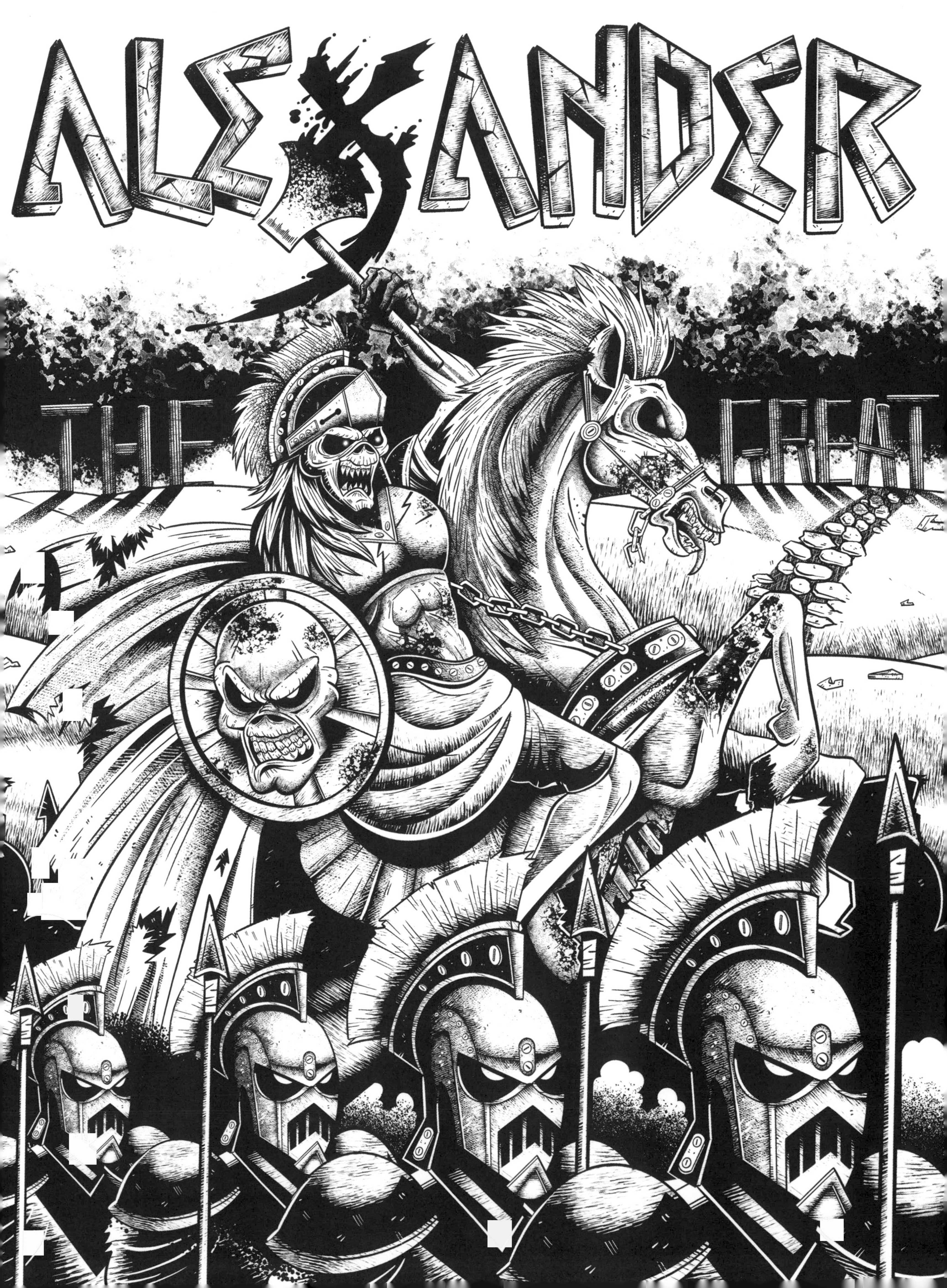
ALEXANDER
THE GREAT

LISTEN WITH NICKO

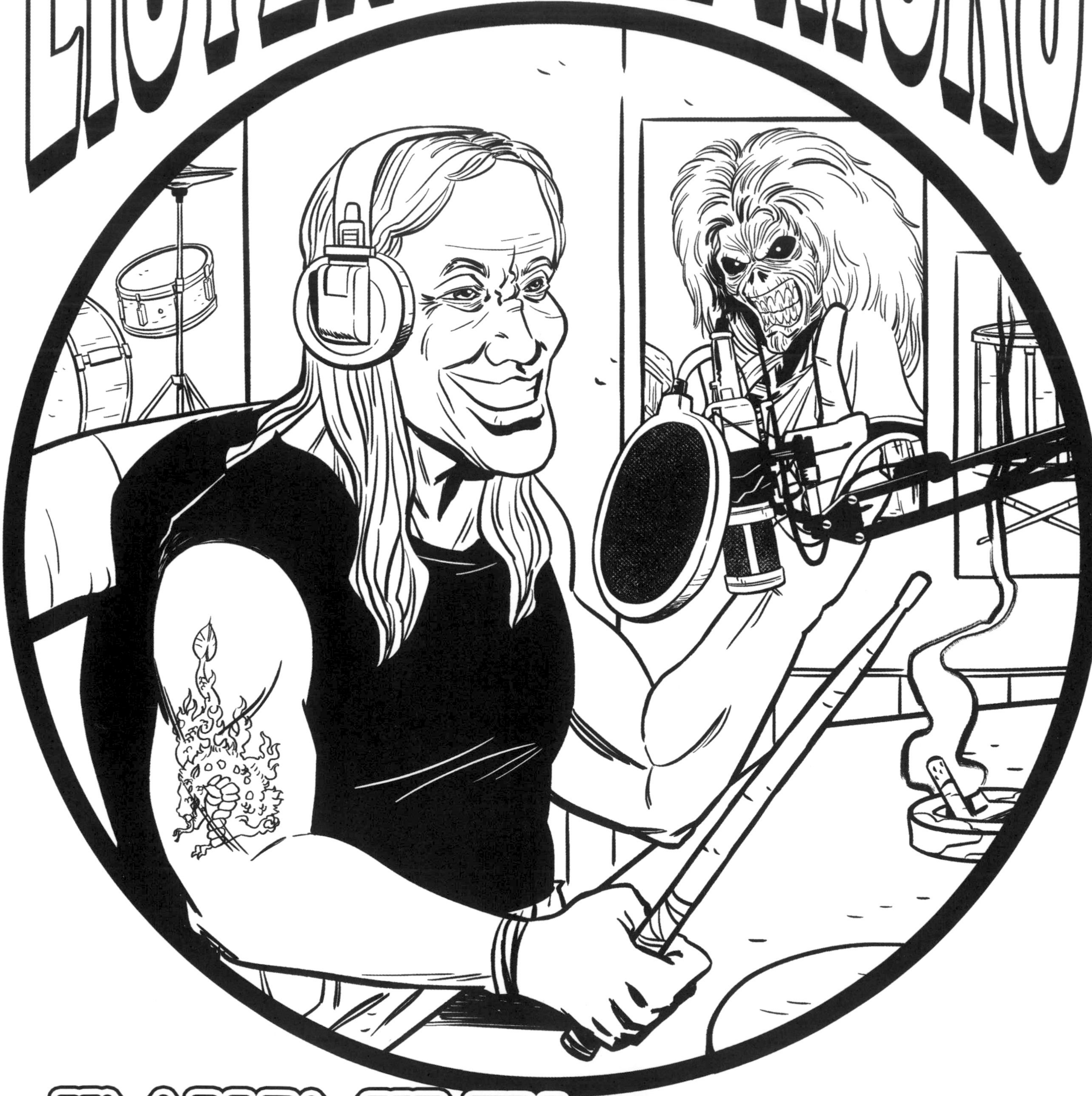

IRON MAIDEN ON YOUR RADIO

BROADCASTING LIVE FROM ANOTHER PLANET

LEAVE YOUR NAME, YOUR NUMBER, ALL THAT MUMBO JUMBO.

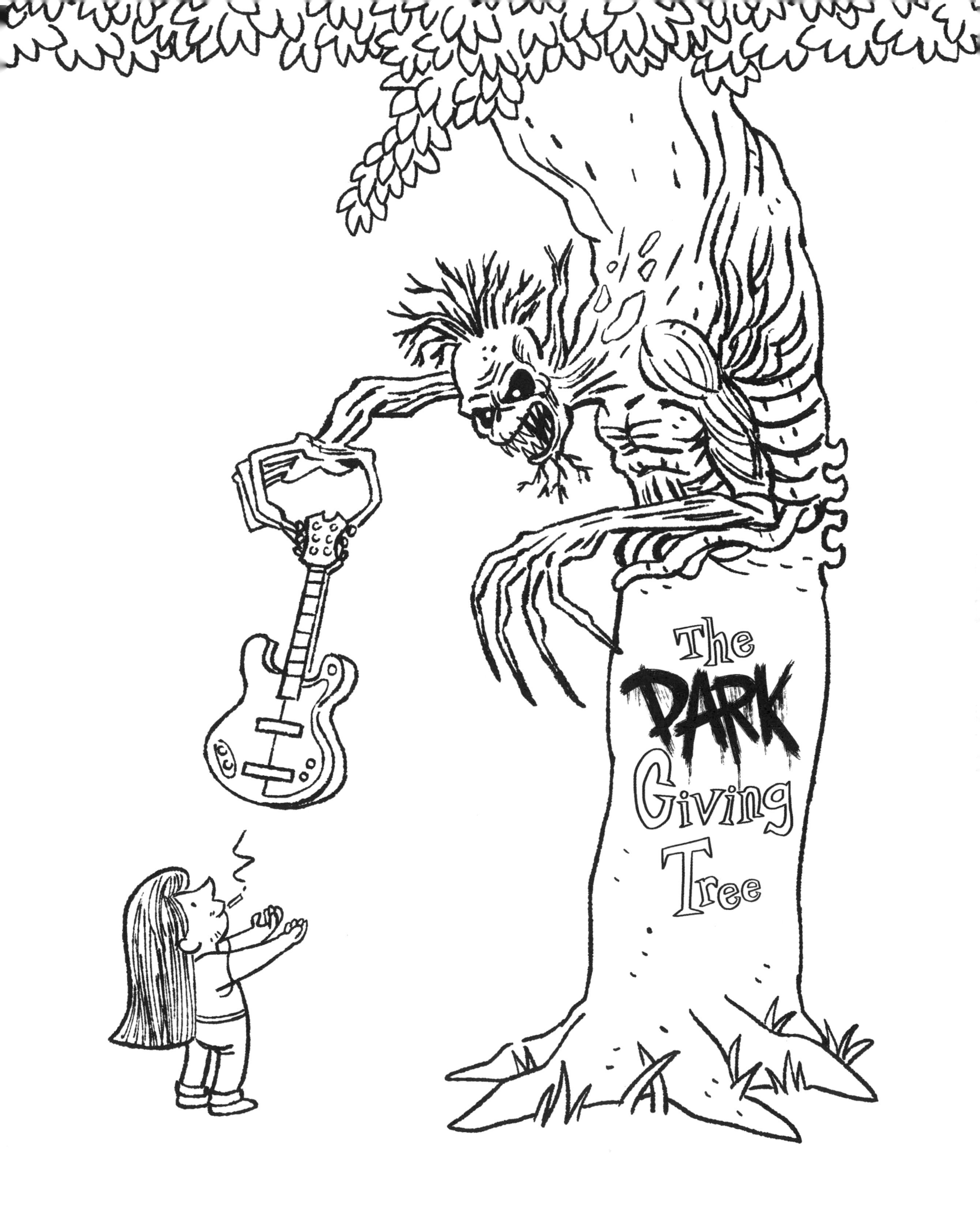
The
DARK
Giving
Tree

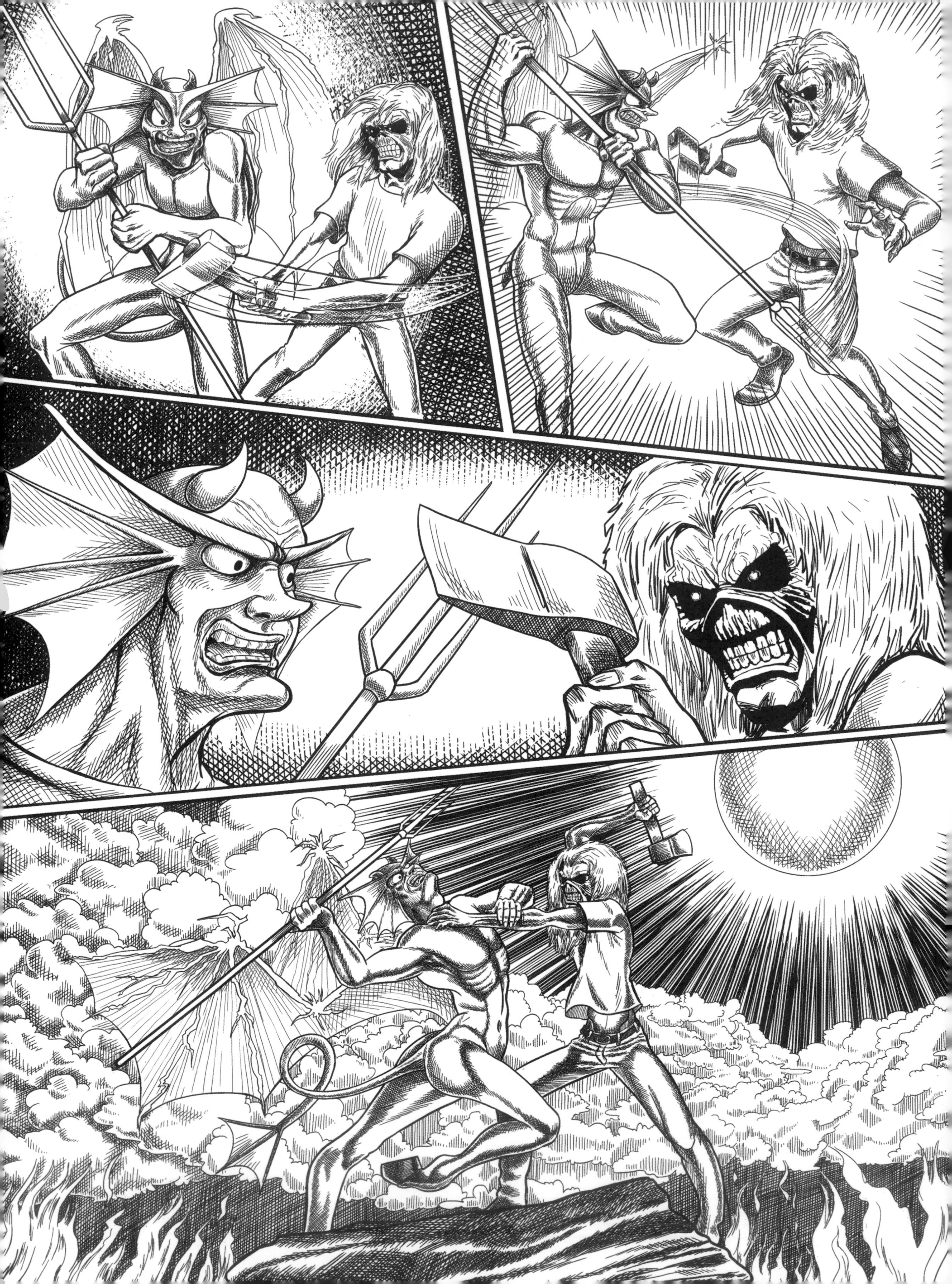

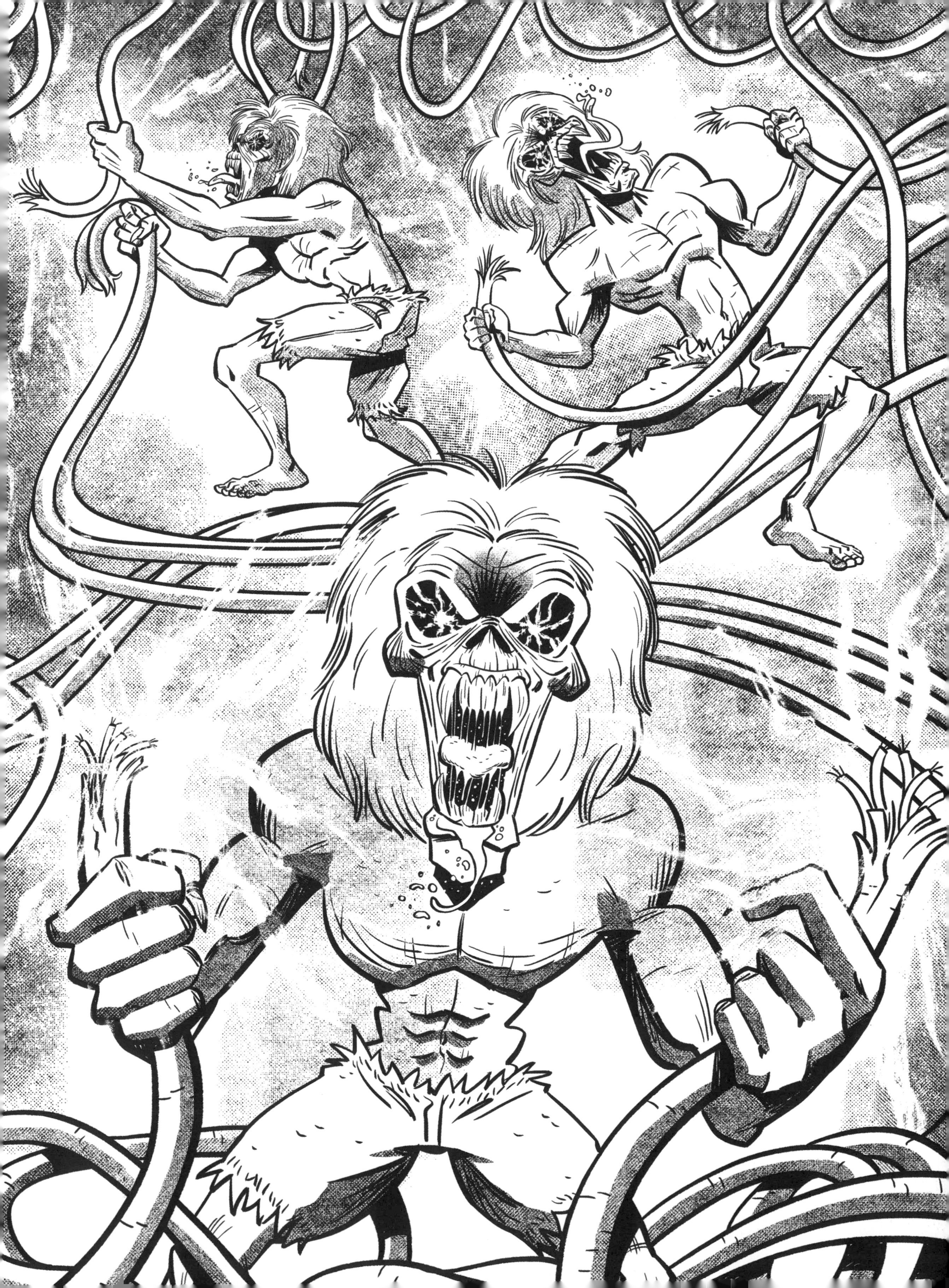

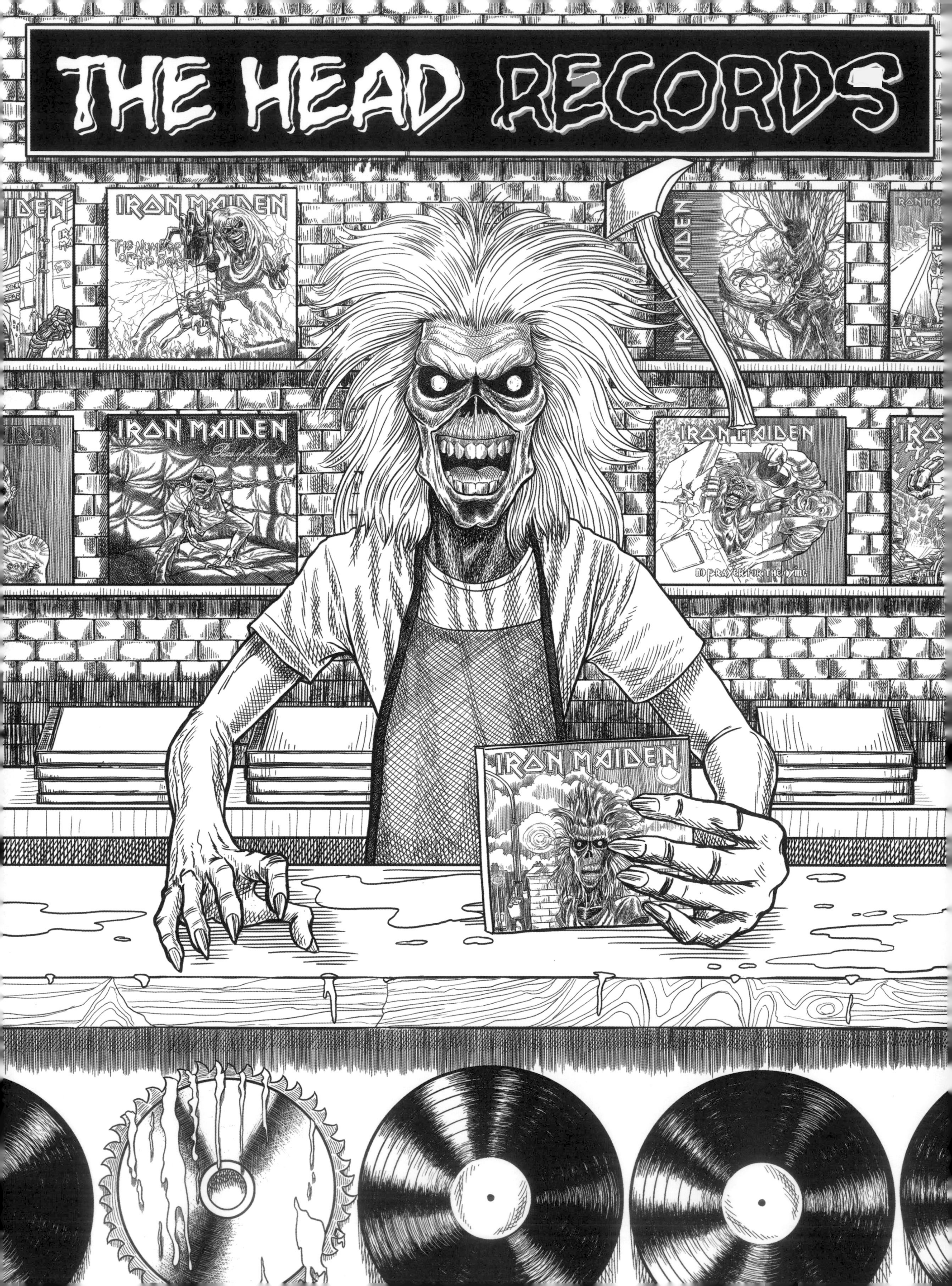

THE HEAD RECORDS
IRON MAIDEN
The Number of the Beast
IRON MAIDEN
IRON MAIDEN
NO PRAYER FOR THE DYING
IRON MAIDEN

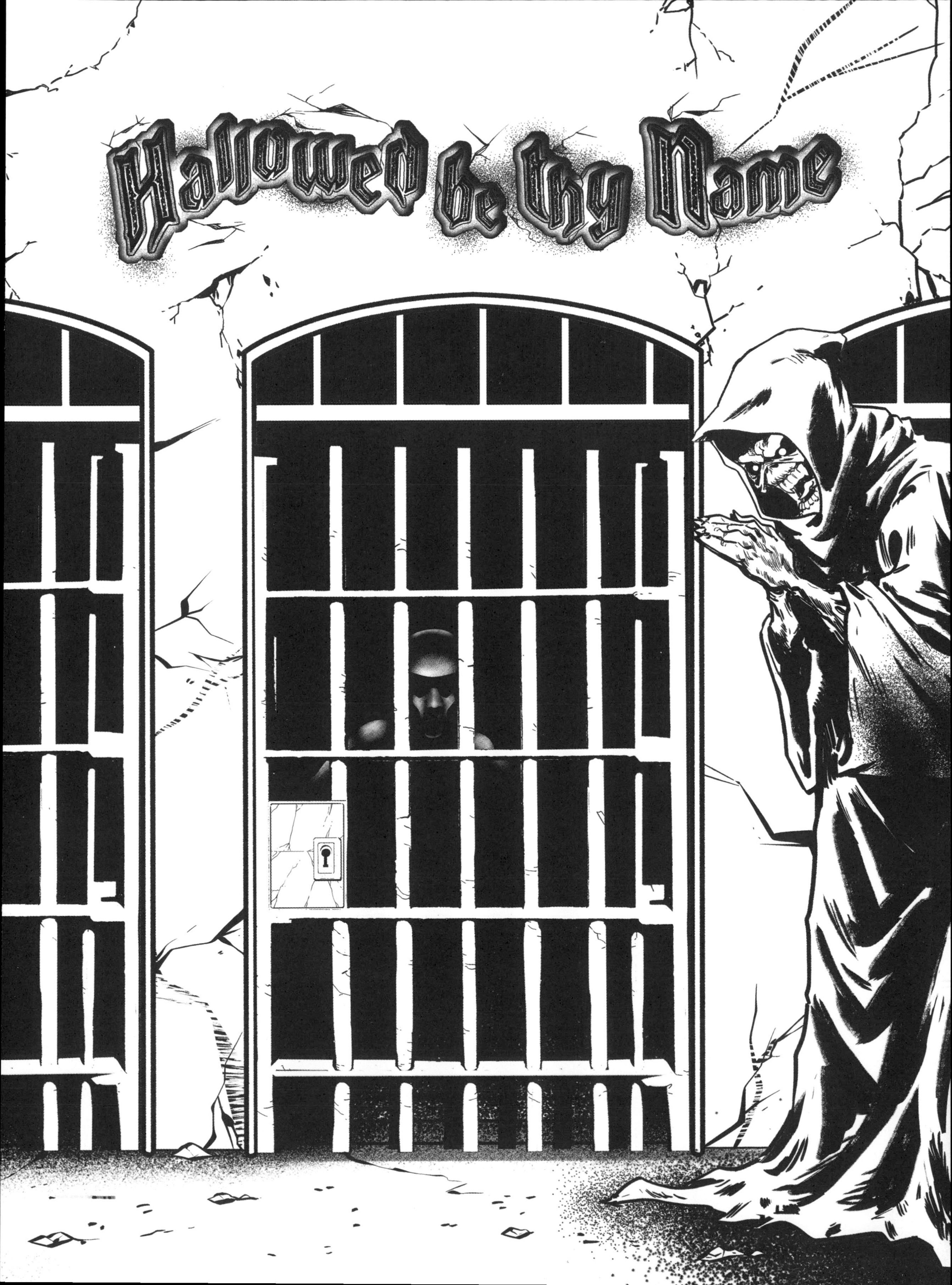
Hallowed be thy Name

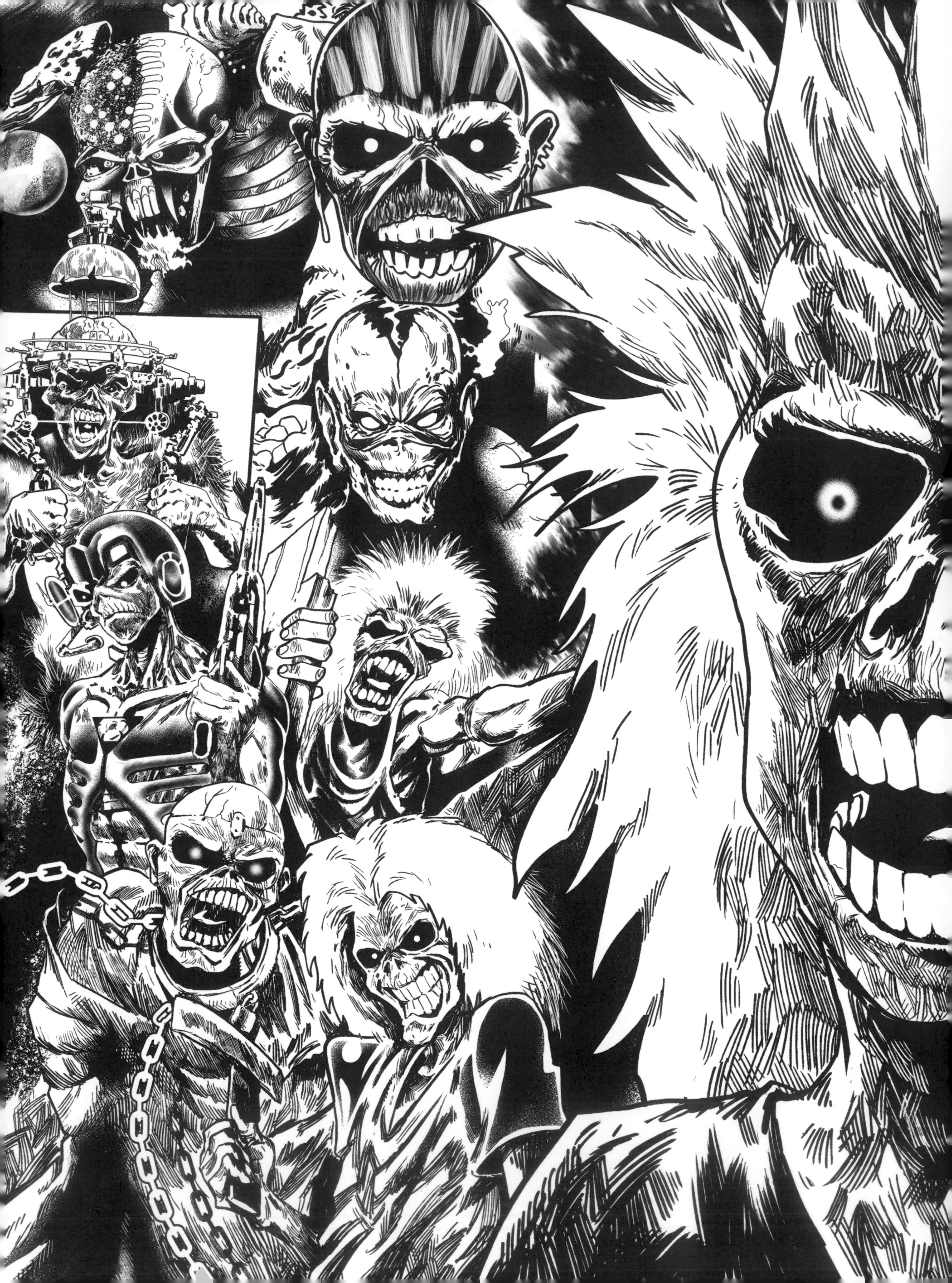

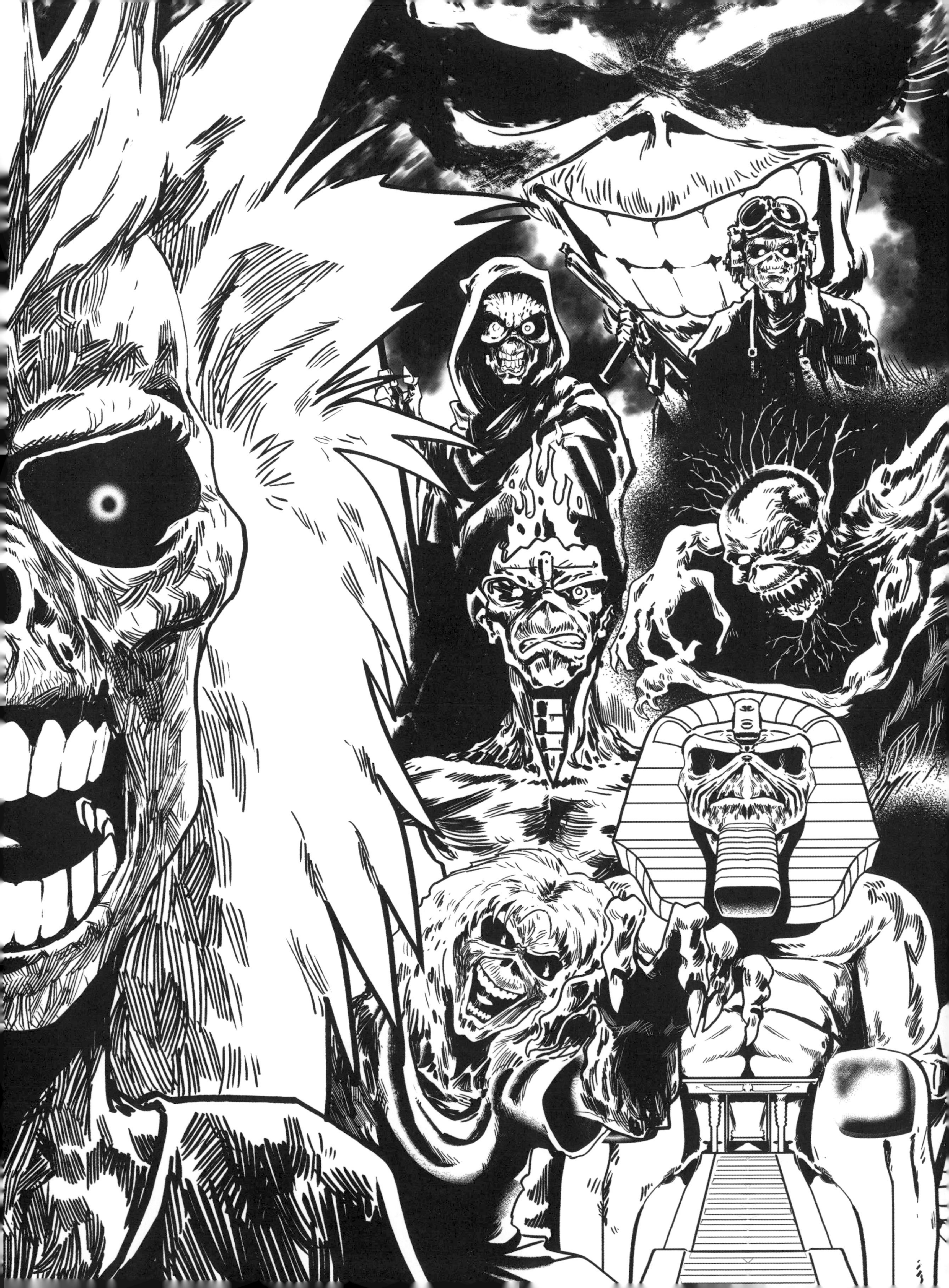

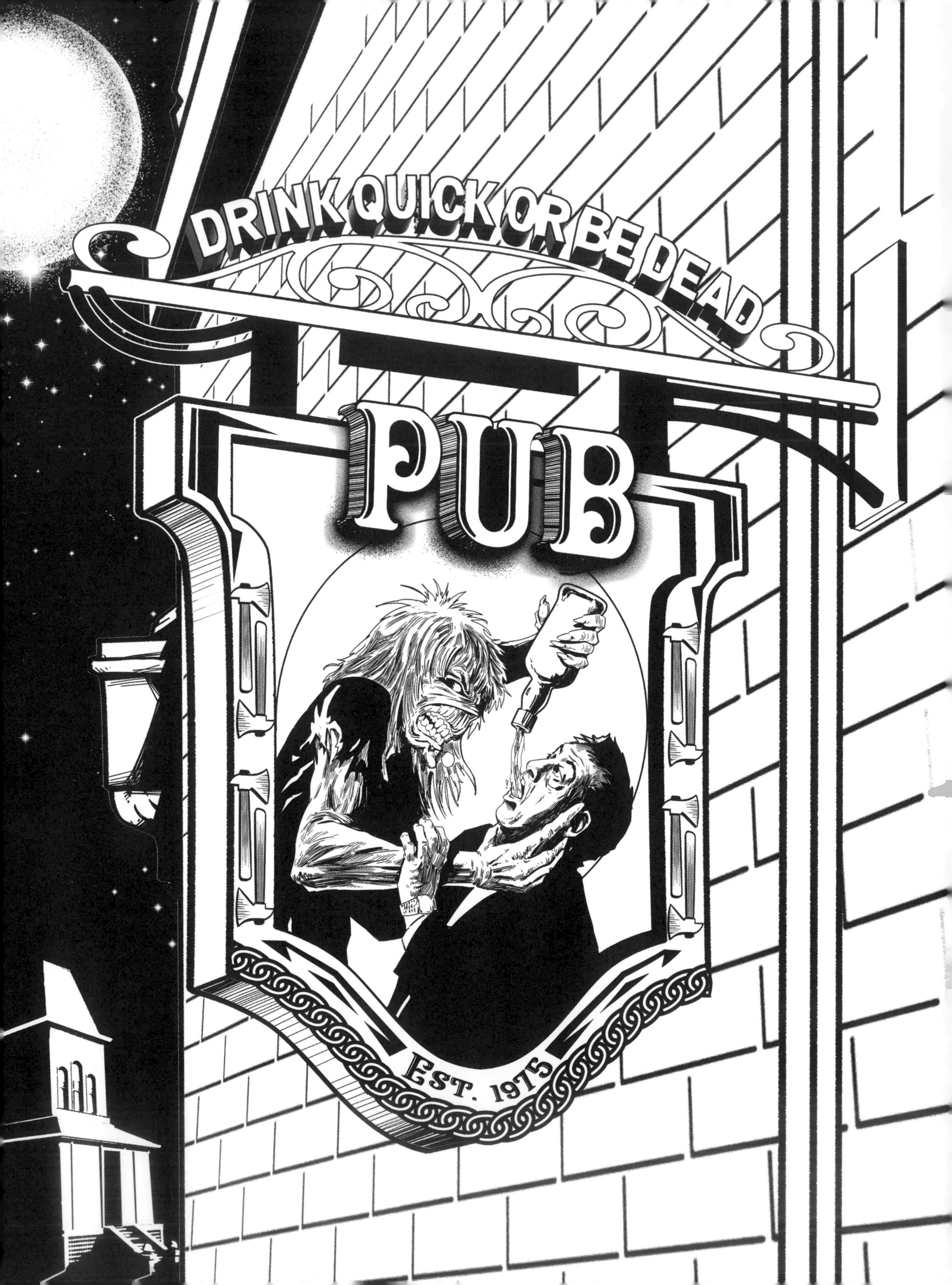
DRINK QUICK OR BE DEAD
PUB
EST. 1975

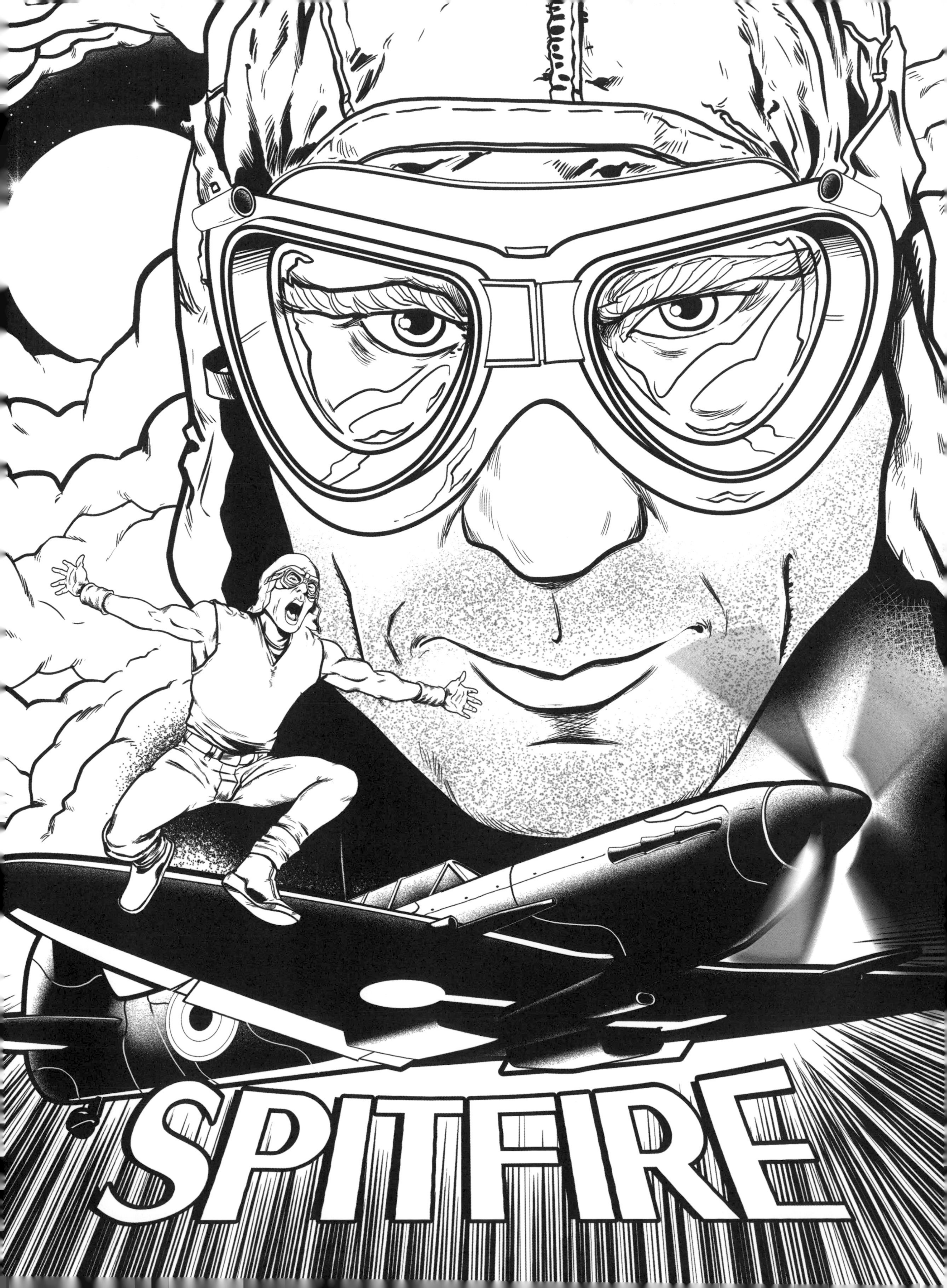
SPITFIRE

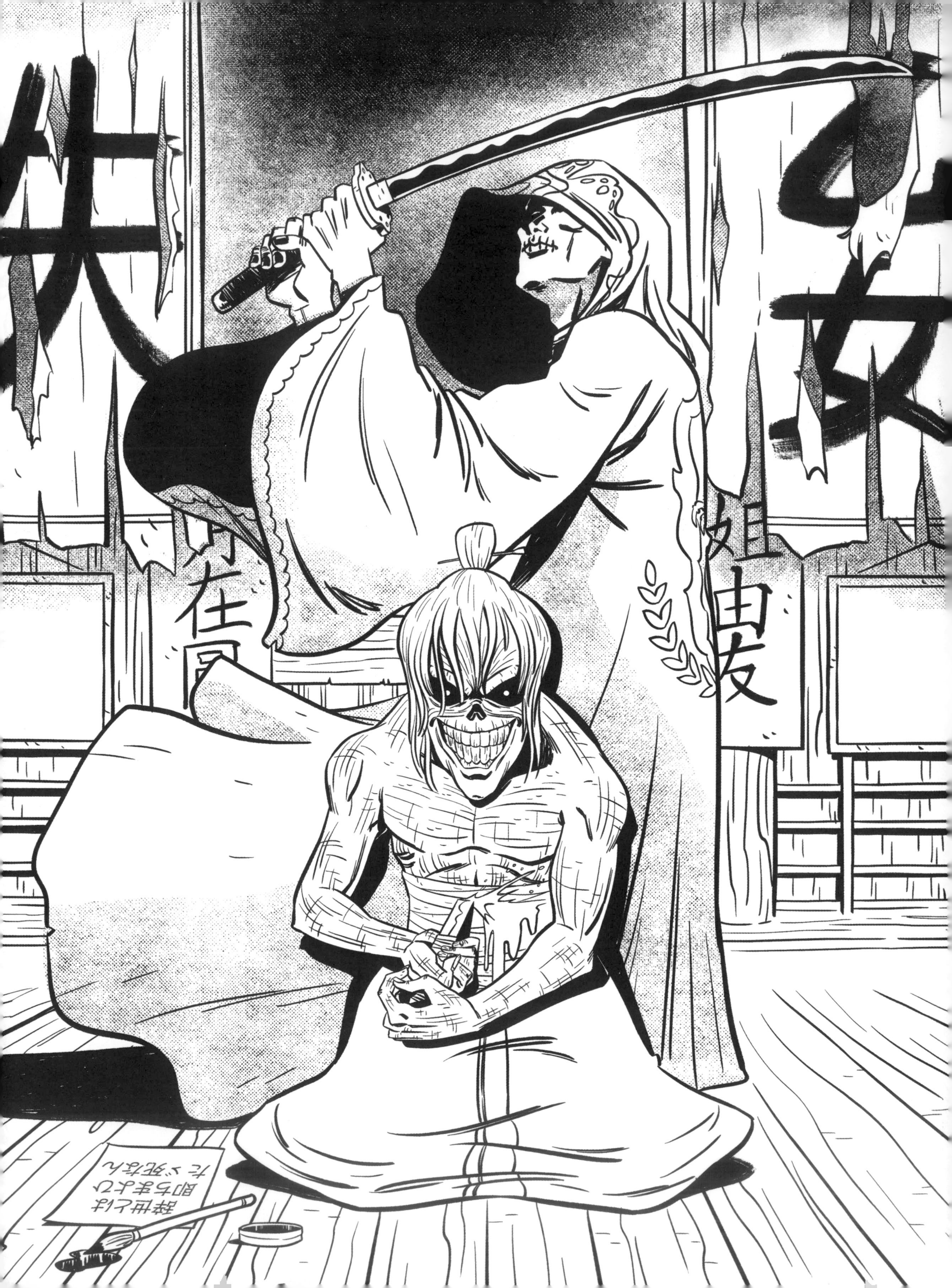
辞世とは
即ちまよひ
たゞ死なん

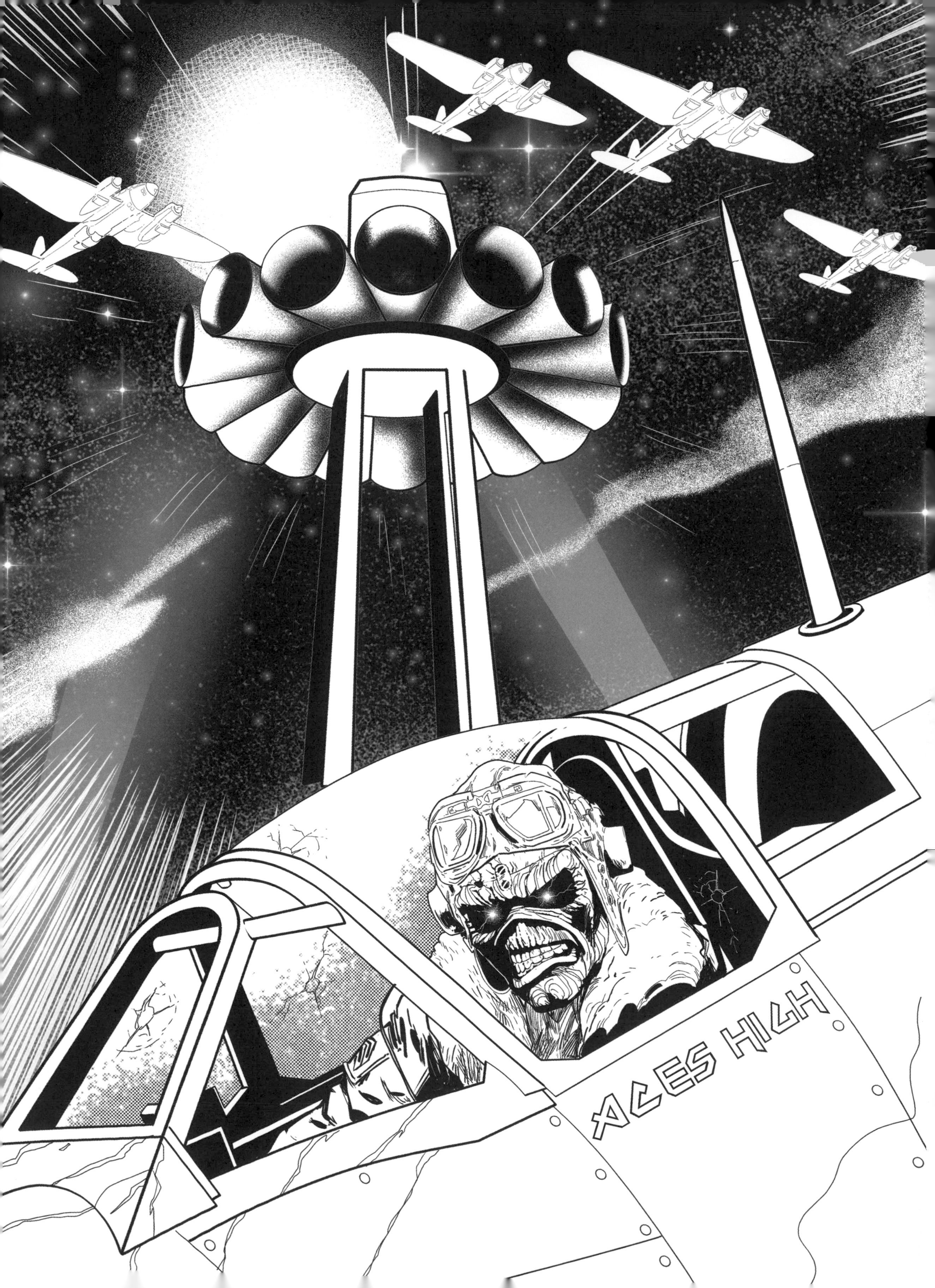
ACES HIGH

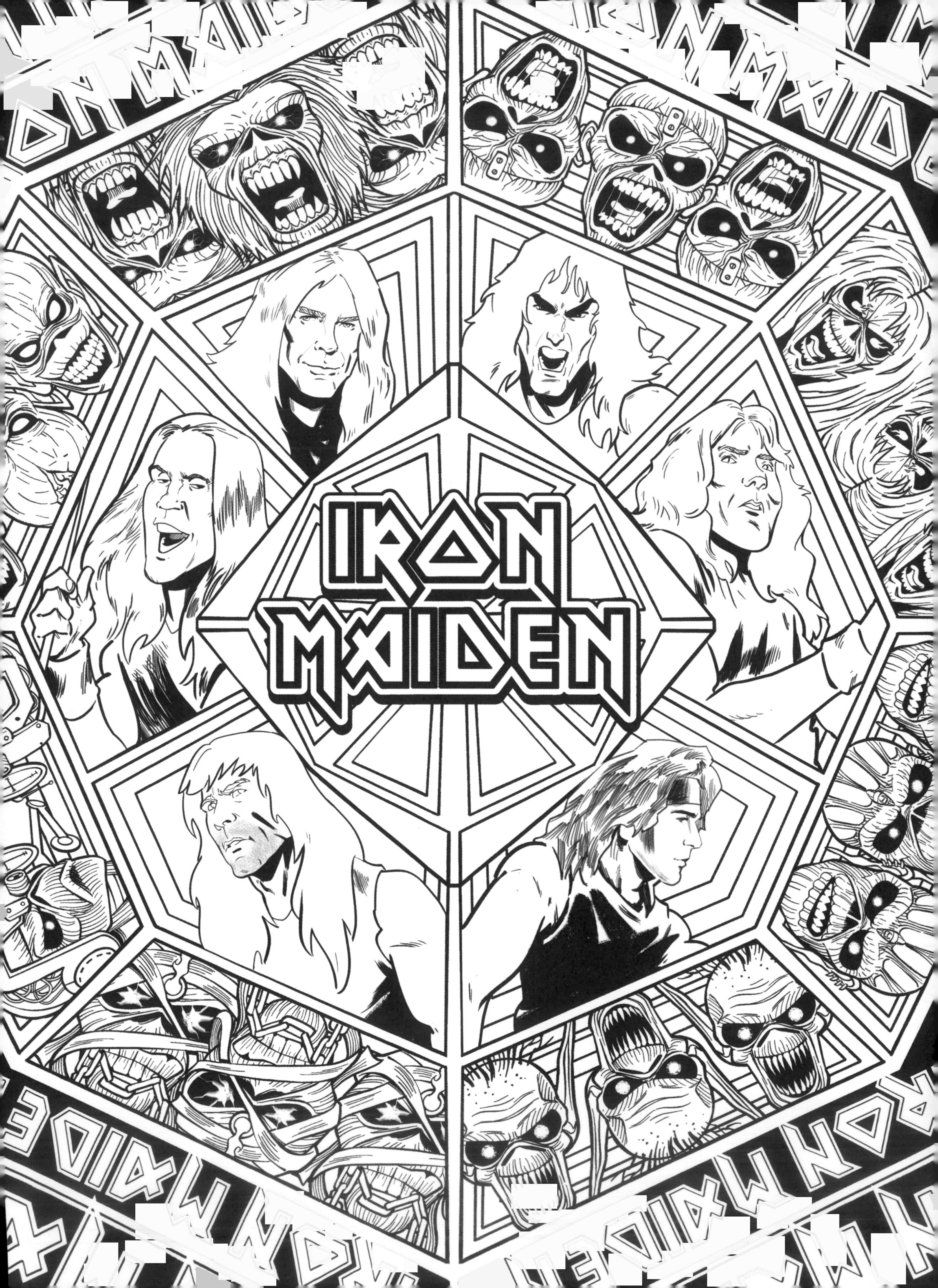
IRON
MAIDEN